Animal

Focus on Contemporary Issues (FOCI) addresses the pressing problems, ideas and debates of the new millennium. Subjects are drawn from the arts, sciences and humanities, and are linked by the impact they have had or are having on contemporary culture. FOCI books are intended for an intelligent, alert audience with a general understanding of, and curiosity about, the intellectual debates shaping culture today. Instead of easing readers into a comfortable awareness of particular fields, these books are combative. They offer points of view, take sides and are written with passion.

SERIES EDITORS
Barrie Bullen and Peter Hamilton

Animal

ERICA FUDGE

REAKTION BOOKS

To Osian and Oran

Published by Reaktion Books Ltd
33 Great Sutton Street
London EC1V ODX, UK

www.reaktionbooks.co.uk

First published 2002
Transferred to digital printing 2010

Series design by Libanus Press

Printed and bound by Chicago University Press

British Library Cataloguing in Publishing Data
Fudge, Erica L
    Animal. – (FOCI)
    1. Human-animal relationships
    2. Animals in art. 3. Animals in literature
    I. Title
    306.4

ISBN 978 1 86189 134 1

Contents

Introduction

Animals present a challenge to humans. They are both similar to and different from us. That is, they are like us – they form bonds, communicate with each other, some of them, like some of us, even manage monogamy – but they are simultaneously completely lost to us. In our fantasies a Dr Dolittle comes along and offers to translate for us, but in reality we know that, hard as we might try, we can never really learn to speak 'dog', let alone understand it when we hear it barked. It is this paradox of like and not like, same and different, that exists in our fascination with animals. But there is also something else; something, perhaps, just as compelling as this desire for communication. The German philosopher Walter Benjamin wrote:

> In an aversion to animals the predominant feeling is fear of being recognized by them through contact. The horror that stirs deep in man is an obscure awareness that in him something lives so akin to the animal that it might be recognized. All disgust is originally disgust at touching. Even when the feeling is mastered, it is only

by a drastic gesture that overleaps its mark: the nauseous is violently engulfed, eaten, while the zone of finest epidermal contact remains taboo. Only in this way is the paradox of the moral demand to be met, exacting simultaneously the overcoming and the subtlest elaboration of man's sense of disgust. He may not deny his bestial relationship with animals, the invocation of which revolts him: he must make himself its master.[1]

Alongside and sometimes working against the desire for communication persists, as Benjamin argues, a fear, and this fear manifests itself as disgust. The disgust is directed towards animals, but it might be fair to see the disgust as being *about* humans, about ourselves. We are horrified that there is a kinship between us and them (a kinship that we have, of course, in part produced through our own desires), and we wish to wipe it out; annihilate it. Mastery – control, domination – is the means by which we annihilate the fear. But if we place these two simultaneous drives – desire for communication and fear – together, as I think we must in our relationships with animals, what emerges is not so much the problem of the animal, as the problem of the human.

We live with animals, we recognize them, we even name some of them, but at the same time we use them as if they were inanimate, as if they were objects. The illogic of this relationship is one that, on a day-to-day basis, we choose to evade, even refuse to acknowledge as present. We, or so we argue, have access to a truth, knowledge, reason and order, into which we place animals. And yet at the heart of that truth, knowledge, reason and order persists this danger, this limitation on our power. Animals are present all of the time in our lives, but frequently we treat them as if they were not there as animals. They are the limit case, if you like, of all of our structures of understanding. They stand between us and our sense of ourselves, but they also allow us to think about ourselves.

This contradiction is the reason for this book. It won't attempt to explain animals, rather, it will attempt to look at the ways in which we live with, think with and use them. Not only are animals both like and not like us, they are also friend and foe, individualized and dissected, loved and eaten; and it is these apparent oppositions that I am interested in here. Because of its size, this book cannot, and does not, attempt to cover everything about our relationships with animals at the beginning of the twenty-first century. Rather than, for example, attempting a detailed analysis of animals in literature, I have chosen a few texts to look at. It is hoped that you will be able to think of many others, and construct for yourself ways of making meaning out of them. Similarly, when discussing an important issue like meat-eating, a couple of examples – rabbit pie and the export of live veal calves – are used to offer some way of thinking about the issue. This is not the place to find a detailed analysis of the nature and history of vegetarianism, although references will point readers to where they might find such studies.

Having said, then, what the book is not, it is worth thinking about what it is. I will not make any direct attempt to proselytize, or present an 'evangelical' reading of animal rights. Rather, I will be asking you, through the organization of the book, to think about the ways in which Western society uses animals. The book is, though, polemical: that is, it presents an argument about the need to rethink our relationships with animals. This polemic arises from an analysis, not of philosophical positions about animals, but of the ways we currently live with them. That is, the book argues that if the variety of ways in which animals are present in Western culture are juxtaposed then the inherent contradictions will ask a number of questions.

In our juxtapositions we have, for example, on the one hand, the close bond that is formed between the owner and the pet, on the other the consumption of animal flesh at the dinner table. Similarly, we have the anthropomorphic representation of animals in classic children's books like *Charlotte's Web* and *The Wind in the Willows*, while at the same time vivisection asserts the absolute difference of the moral positions of humans and animals. It is these contradictions – and others – that are constantly in play in our relations with animals, but are often forgotten: we rarely make the connection between the cat we live with and the cow we eat. But by bringing these contradictions to the fore I hope that this book might continue the debate about the ways in which we live with animals in the twenty-first century.

But it is not only contemporary culture that will be the focus here. The history of many of the ways in which we currently live with animals offers some sobering reminders that those ways have a source; that is, that they are not natural. It is also included to remind us that many of our apparently friendly gestures towards other species are grounded in a firm belief in human superiority rather than a concept of animal 'worth'. For example, the outlawing of dog-carts (carts pulled by dogs) in nineteenth-century London did not announce a new understanding of the rights of animals; rather it was a response to human displeasure at the very visible nature of animal abuse on the streets and to human disgust at the perceived pollution from animal dirt and disease. What might appear to be a movement to increase the welfare of animals is simultaneously a movement to shield humans from the use of animals that was – and is – so prevalent in our societies. When the dog-carts were banned, the dogs used to pull them did not retire to spend the rest of their days happily lying by the hearth. Most of them were killed; they were too expensive to maintain as pets.[2] What on the surface appears to be a gesture based upon kindness is also a gesture of human self-preservation. As Benjamin argued, our greatest fear of animals is through contact – and I would include contact through the eyes, ears, nose and mouth, as well as through touch – and the only way we have to overcome this fear and disgust is through mastery. He proposes eating as the most violent means by which animals are 'engulfed' by humans, but we might include other ways in which we consume animals: through experimenting upon, caging, hunting, representing, wearing them (this list could go on). By invoking history alongside contemporary debates our current relations with animals become less and less straightforward, and many assumptions that have become wholly naturalized in our cultures are made strange.

So what is it that is naturalized? In her book *Reordering the Natural World* the anthropologist Annabelle Sabloff has proposed, following the work of George Lakoff and Mark Johnson, that we live by metaphors. That is, that metaphor, the figure of speech whereby aspects of one thing are applied to another, is one of the key organizing structures whereby our lives are given meaning. An example of a metaphor might be 'Peter's a pig.' In this metaphor we know that Peter is not actually a pig, but that he has some of the qualities that we associate with pigs – greediness, dirtiness and so on. For the literary critic Norman Friedman the relationship between Peter and the pig is 'based on likeness in difference'.[3] This is where the metaphor works; it brings both of the ideas – Peter and pig – together and creates something that is more than just a mixture of the two. We do not have a crossbreed, if you like, but a new way of looking at an existing species.

Sabloff writes: 'Metaphor, that unstoppable faculty of the human mind to make associations, most often between an experienced and named domain of life and an apprehended but unnamed domain, is a fundamental mechanism for the patterning of cognitive and behavioural practice and emotional life.' We look at the unknown and name it through our experience of the known: we, to use Friedman's phrase, base our understanding on its likeness in difference to ourselves. What is incomprehensible becomes knowable through its translation from thing 'out there' to metaphor 'in here'. Sabloff proposes three key metaphors by which we live with animals, those distinct and different creatures. In the domestic domain the metaphor is one of kinship: animals are represented as members of our families; in what she terms the factory domain, animals are figured as artefacts, tools, objects for our use; and in the rhetoric of animal rights, they are perceived as citizens.[4] In each of these cases animals as such disappear and are replaced by a metaphorical structure that attempts to represent what is, for humans, unobtainable.

What is absent, Sabloff argues, in our current mode of thinking about animals is another metaphor that would allow for a biocentric, as opposed to anthropocentric, relationship, a metaphor that would allow for 'the radical otherness of other life forms, that is, their inherent value outside the human ethical domain' to be acknowledged, as opposed to a relation that sees only humans as centrally significant, and represents the world accordingly. This new metaphor, she argues, would provide the foundation for a new lived relation. Sabloff is certainly right to argue that we lack a language at present in which we can think about and represent animals to ourselves *as animals*, in ways that are not metaphorical. But I am not sure that the way forward is through the creation of another metaphor – what she calls a 'practical poetry' – by which we can live with meaning in 'a more benign, respectful relationship with our habitats', and with animals.[5] Creating a new way of representing and thinking about the natural world might allow the old relations to persist. Rather than attempting to find a new metaphor, then, what I think is necessary is a relocation of the ways in which we live with animals on a day-to-day basis. The argument of this book is that if we acknowledge some of the – frequently cruel – contradictions in the ways in which we live with and think about animals we might be on the road to creating a new language. The language will not precede the lived relation, a renewed acquaintance with the lived relation will, I hope, help us to create another language.

But, if the lived relation is so contradictory it is probably worth pausing to consider how it came to be lived as true, as natural in the first place. How is it that we haven't really – as societies rather than as individuals – sat back and thought about the problems inherent in our relationships with animals? How come, to return to Walter Benjamin, wearing metaphorical gloves is all that we have needed to protect ourselves from the terror of contact?

One starting point is what, in Western culture, has been, and for many still is, regarded as the beginning, Genesis. It might be argued that, in multicultural societies such as our own, where different religious beliefs exist alongside each other, and alongside atheism, beginning with the Christian myth is a rather limited and limiting way into a more general discussion of animals. My defence is that within European and North American cultures (and this is what is under discussion here) our legislation and institutions are, whether we like it or not, often premised upon Christian ideas. Much of the naturalized morality of our cultures comes from this source, and this is, I think, particularly the case with our relations to animals.

According to Genesis 1, the creation took six days, and those days represented the six stages of the universe. Beginning with the heaven and the earth, day and night on the first day, God ended his work with Adam and Eve on the sixth. God began with the basis, the foundation of his creation, and ended with a creature formed in his own image. Humanity was the final and greatest of God's creations, and so humans, created after the animals, were given dominion over them. That is, as one seventeenth-century commentator noted, man (and it was *man*) was 'a petty God . . . all things being put in subjection under his feet'.[6] As God had absolute power over Adam, so Adam had absolute power over the animals. This power was made manifest in Genesis 1:19, when Adam named the animals: 'and whatsoever Adam called every living creature, that was the name thereof'. It is as if the animals had no identity, no presence without Adam, and their inherent powerlessness, perhaps most easily described as their inability to name themselves, has persisted in human relations with animals. An animal cannot think, we argue, and therefore it is down to us to think for it. If we firmly believed that a cow could think like us it would become very difficult to justify eating it. Instead, we decide that a cow can't think as we understand the term, and that it is therefore morally acceptable to eat the cow. In these terms, dominion is a claim for the human right – even duty – to treat animals as objects of use rather than as fellow subjects of the planet.

From this notion of man's absolute dominion over the natural world comes the faith – also naturalized in much contemporary culture – in anthropocentrism; the belief that the human (*anthropos* is the Greek term for human) is the centre of all things, that the world revolves around him (feminists have spent many years attempting to turn that him into him/her). The Christian narrative has had a massive impact on the ways humans relate to the world around them. Anthropocentrism is naturalized: the eating of meat – often undertaken without thought for what it is that is really being eaten – is just one example of how normal anthropocentrism is in our cultures. Cannibalism, on the other hand, has always been the source of horror and comment, and not because of the flavour of human flesh.

I am not, of course, the first person to see the Christian narrative as lying at the heart of our relations with animals. This belief has persisted throughout Western history, and was brought to the fore in 1967 when Lynn White Jr wrote a now famous article in the journal *Science* entitled 'The Historical Roots of our Ecological Crisis'. In this article White laid the blame for many environmental catastrophes firmly at the door of Christianity. He wrote, 'Christianity is the most anthropocentric religion the world has seen.' The original impetus for developments in science and technology, which to his mind had produced environmental catastrophes of numerous kinds, should, he argued, be traced to the Christian belief that a knowledge of God would be increased by a knowledge of his creation. White argued that 'Christianity bears a huge burden of guilt' for the ways in which we relate to – and use – the natural world. It has given us a reason, or perhaps an excuse, for many of our most destructive actions. For White, the Christian narrative was not merely a myth of origin, it had much more import than that.[7]

Eight years later F. B. Welbourn wrote a response to White's article in which he argued that far from reinforcing notions of human dominion, the Christian relation to the natural world, symbolized in Adam's naming of the animals, did something rather different. He wrote: 'By the act of naming the animals man recognized his responsibility towards them.'[8] This interpretation of the Bible presented humans as stewards rather than as masters or rulers of the natural world. With power, Welbourn argued, comes responsibility. It is our duty to shepherd rather than dominate nature.

The difference between dominion and stewardship, between human rights to use, and human duty to act responsibly, will be traced throughout this book. In many places it is clear that it is a matter of interpretation which of the relations is being exercised. Many of us, myself included, find it difficult to see all human relations with animals as being based upon dominion, but it is often worth thinking about whether those relations that we see as based on the more generous model of stewardship really are. The zoo is a good way of thinking about this. Many zoos now claim their status as conservation organizations, the protectors of endangered species. This would place them as stewards of animals. But there remains an alternative reading, based, perhaps, on the links that have been made between zoos and the contexts in which they first emerged: animals displayed as evidence of the West's 'conquest' of the 'barbaric' world.[9] There is a possibility of reading zoos as places where animals are imprisoned for the benefit only of human entertainment, and this would make the relation between humans and other species witnessed in the zoo one of dominion. It might sound like merely a matter of opinion, something upon which we can agree to differ, but I hope that by presenting the possibility of alternative ways of thinking about how we live with animals this book will unsettle some of the commonsense assumptions that prevail in our cultures.

What is certain in both of the interpretations of the zoo – and in both of the interpretations of the Bible – is that the human remains central: as either preserver or conqueror and observer. Animals are merely the means by which we exercise our power, and this is where, I think, Christian ideas are so central to the ways in which we co-exist with animals. These ideas have made natural – to the extent that we no longer need the knowledge of Christianity itself to support such naturalization – our current relations with them. But there is a possibility of breaking out of this: if, as we put on leather shoes, we begin to think about the animal from which the leather came, and to recognize the kind of stories we tell ourselves to make it acceptable to wear them, then we are, perhaps, beginning to take those stories as just that: stories. From this basis it is possible to begin to seek another way of thinking.[10]

But, of course, Christianity is not the only faith practised in the West. Other religions exist side by side with Christianity in our cultures, and some of them offer alternative relations to animals that are worth pausing briefly to think about. In the *Qur'an*, for example, is written, 'there is not an animal . . . in the earth, nor a creature flying on two wings, but they are peoples [or communities] like you'. As James L. Westcoat Jr has argued, 'communities of animals praise Allah through their existence and their actions. They have souls (*nafs*) of various types and qualities that constitute essential parts of the world soul. Some Muslim scholars infer from this passage that animals will be resurrected on the day of judgement along with humans.' However, as Westcoat also notes, 'at the same time, the *Qur'an* states that animals are subordinate to human beings and that they are created to serve human beings'.[11] They are simultaneously the same and other – us and them.

This is a paradox that we can also trace in what is apparently one of the most obvious challenges to the kind of human rule espoused in the Bible and the *Qur'an*: that which comes from Buddhism. This Eastern religion, now practised throughout the world, offers a radically different relationship with animals. At the heart of Buddhism is the belief in rebirth, in the understanding that death is not an ending, but a new beginning, with the soul reborn in another form. The nature of that form – whether human or animal, male or female – depends to a large extent of the nature of the life lived by the deceased. A pure life will lead to a higher form in the next life, and the most pure life, one that included enlightenment and understanding, can lead to rebirth in 'a Pure Land'. For all believers, however, there is a recognition that the relationship with all other living beings is crucial. The first precept of Buddhism is the 'most important', and it is, as Peter Harvey terms it, 'the resolution not to kill or injure any human, animal, bird, fish or insect'. Kindness and compassion to all other living beings are at the heart of Buddhism in a way that cannot necessarily be claimed of the Christian faith (although an individual such as St Francis of Assisi might have disputed this).

One of the key reasons for this different relation with animals is the sense in Buddhism that 'no permanent self or I exists within a person'. Harvey proposes that Buddhist teaching does not 'support a positive regard for persons as unique entities, as do Christian teachings'. The belief in past (and future) lives means that the clear dividing line between humans and animals present in Christian faith cannot exist: in Buddhism '"your" suffering and "my" suffering are not inherently different'.[12] This link between humans and animals is absent in Christianity: Adam is active: he gives names; the animals passive: they were named. Adam, if you like, is a subject, the animals objects.

However, underlying Buddhism's sense of a link between human and animal lives is a key difference between them. Animals are regarded as lower beings by degree. It is into the form of an animal that a person who has led an impure life will be reborn: animals exist as a kind of punishment. So while there is a link between humans and animals – an animal may have been human in a past life, a human may become an animal in a future life – there remains a sense of superiority and inferiority. Humans are at the top while animals, as Florin Deleanu has written, 'cannot develop liberating insight and progress along the Buddhist Path'.[13] Once again, at the point where similarity appears to emerge, gloves are put on, a division is installed.

However, the sense of the link between human and animal that lies at the core of Buddhism can also be found in another very different challenge to human superiority. This time the text is not religious but, for some, anti-religious. In 1859 Charles Darwin's *The Origin of Species* was first published. In this work he argued that the new discoveries being made by geologists about the age of the earth meant that new ways of understanding the living creatures on the planet were needed. The creation narrative of the Bible was no longer credible, as the earth was much older than any arithmetical analysis of the Scriptures could propose, and what Darwin put forward instead of the Christian creation myth was the theory of evolution. The outcome of this theory was a world in which nature was never static, in which creatures (and he included human beings in this) were not created in their final state, but had evolved to become what they now were, and would, by implication, continue to evolve.

Evolution is a response to environment. The struggle for survival meant that the fittest survived, as the fittest were often in possession of faculties that made their survival more likely. For Darwin, adaptation to environment was vital, and did not happen in a generation: it took place over millions of years. One of his proposals was that originally there was perhaps only one species, but to survive that one species had to divide and specialize: some creatures adapting to living in the water, others in the air and so on. After millions and millions of years the natural world had evolved to become the diverse and astonishing one that Darwin saw before him. As he wrote at the end of *The Origin of Species*: 'There is a grandeur in this view of life, with its several powers, having been originally breathed into a few forms or into one; and that, whilst this planet has gone cycling on according to the fixed law of gravity, from so simple a beginning endless forms most beautiful and most wonderful have been, and are being, evolved.'[14] Far from ending the mystery of nature Darwin's theory placed that mystery in a different context. Here was not the inscrutable nature of God, rather it was the extraordinary wonder of nature itself.

What Darwin's theory proposed, then, was an end to human distinction: an end to the separation of man from beast. It was impossible, following his scheme, that humans should have ever existed as a breed apart. Instead, humans were animals, just the most evolved species. The Christian narrative of superiority and dominion was seemingly destroyed in one movement, a destruction that was most infamously recognized at a meeting of the British Association on 30 June 1860. Here Thomas Henry Huxley, speaking in support of the Darwinist position, was confronted by 'Soapy Sam', Samuel Wilberforce, the Bishop of Oxford, himself an acclaimed amateur naturalist. The meeting was regarded as a landmark victory for Darwinism, and the following exchange (or a version of it) has become a legend in the history of science:

Wilberforce: Is it on your grandfather's or your grandmother's side that you claim descent from the apes?
Huxley: I would rather be descended from an ape than a bishop.

Wilberforce's attack on Darwin's work was voiced as a response to what he regarded as the latter's attack on human status. Huxley's response was to attack what he regarded as the Bishop's wilful defence of an arrogant and unscientific position. As one contemporary report of the meeting recorded it: Huxley rose in response to the Bishop's question and said that 'He was not ashamed to have a monkey for his ancestor; but he would be ashamed to be connected with a man who used great gifts to obscure the truth.'[15] Truth here is no longer the scriptural truth of Genesis, but a scientific, empirical truth, made clear by the expanding geological record.

Darwin's work, so fundamental to the ways in which many of us understand the natural world now, was shocking in its challenge to the established Christian world view when it appeared. This is a challenge that is still felt. In Kansas in 1997, for example, the 'Board of Education voted to delete virtually every mention of evolution from the state's science curriculum'. And in the same year, a Gallup poll in the US 'found that 40 per cent of those surveyed favoured teaching creationism [an explanation based upon belief in the absolute truth of Genesis] instead of evolution in schools'.[16] What is gone in Darwin's work, and what is maintained in creationism, is the sense of a static nature, with humans on the top rung, and below them apes, and then, by degree, other animals, with no chance of movement between the species. Evolutionary theory proposes in place of this a nature constantly in flux, with no fixed point of perfection.

However, the challenge offered by the theory of evolution was not experienced throughout the world. Where, in America particularly, 'creationism' turned itself into 'Creation Science' to gain credibility,[17] in Japan primatologists accepted evolutionary theory without difficulty. As Frans de Waal has noted, 'to the Buddhist and Confucian mind, both ideas [of evolution and of humans as descendents of apes] are eminently plausible, even likely, and there is nothing insulting about them'. These important religious and cultural differences have, for de Waal, had an impact on the ways in which primates have been understood: 'questions about animal behavior [in Japan] were from the start uncontaminated by feelings of superiority and aversion to the attribution of emotions and intentions that paralysed Western science'.[18] But in the West the impact was far greater: the human, previously a God on earth, was now one among the animals. Dominion, in this world view, must take on a very different meaning. No longer God-given, humanity's rule over the rest of the animals can only be understood as a rule of strength and ingenuity, not right.

But, of course, Darwin's work also offered the possibility of a very different way of thinking about our relation with the natural world. The theory of evolution could be used as a way forward, as a blueprint for a more equal relation. After all, if we share great- (and great-great-. . .) grandparents, we might also think about sharing with animals in ways that a belief in dominion might ignore. In H. G. Wells's 1896 novel *The Island of Dr Moreau*, for example, the horrors and possibilities of the link between humans and animals are brought to one logical conclusion. The vivisector Moreau cuts up animals to make them more human-like, for, as he says, 'it is a possible thing to transplant tissue from one part of an animal to another, or from one animal to another'. He goes on, more terrifyingly, to make the case for not only the possibility of producing animals with bodily likeness to humans, but mental ones as well: 'the possibilities of vivisection do not stop at a mere physical metamorphosis. A pig may be educated. The mental structure is even less determinate than the bodily.'[19] Moreau's animal-men are monstrous creations used by Wells to speak against vivisection. The very possibility of the link between animals and humans reveals how close those groups are and, because of this, vivisection – the absolute objectification of the animal – becomes a nightmare. Cutting up an animal after Darwin can be read as cutting up a relative, a recognition both shocking and, for anti-vivisectionists, potentially productive, as the ethics of experimentation become more and more difficult to uphold.

Dominion cannot persist comfortably, then, with the recognition of sameness, but somehow, in contemporary culture, we manage to live like Moreau: to have an understanding of a shared origin, and shared capacity, but also, and simultaneously, to believe in the human right to dominion. Wells's fable is shocking, but only because it brings to the surface many of the paradoxes of our own relation with animals. While in the process of reading we regard Moreau as the villain, in the process of co-existing in the real world with animals he might actually represent us more fully than the story's narrator, Prendick, who can declare:

Poor brutes! I began to see the viler aspect of Moreau's cruelty. I had not thought before of the pain and trouble that came to these poor victims after they had passed from Moreau's hands. I had shivered only at the days of actual torment in the [vivisection] enclosure. But now that seemed to be the lesser part. Before, they had been beasts, their instincts fitly adapted to their surroundings, and happy as living things may be. Now they stumbled in the shackles of humanity, lived in a fear that never died, fretted by a law they could not understand; their mock-human existence began in an agony, was one long internal struggle, one long dread of Moreau – and for what? It was the wantonness that stirred me.[20]

While most of us may not actually engage in vivisection, most of us do engage in what might be termed metaphorical vivisections. We eat meat and wear fur, for example, but at the same time we recognize the capacity of animals to be more than mere meat and fur-bearers. Like Moreau, we can see the similarities, and we can objectify simultaneously.

What follow here, then, are three chapters, each with a different focus. In the first, questions of visibility and invisibility and their impact on human/animal relations are the focus. The second looks at real and symbolic animals, and particularly at the concept of anthropomorphism, the humanizing of animals. The third chapter has as its focus the question of human power, and this discussion is formulated around the question of intelligence: who has it, and what that possession can bring with it. Finally, I turn to the word 'animal' itself, and think about the ways in which we can (and cannot) think ethically with such a word.

What is at stake ultimately is our own ability to think beyond ourselves, to include within the orbit of our imaginations as well as our material existences, those beings of other species. A failure here creates the ground for the continuation of many of those practices that we would regard as cruel and paradoxical. A failure also reveals a limitation to our own capacity, something that might seem to be at odds with the absolute power that we constantly assert over animals.

CHAPTER ONE

Visible and Invisible: Questions of Recognition

At 11.55 on 31 January 1961, Ham, a four-year-old male chimpanzee, was sent into space. He was, according to NASA reports, 'a really loveable little fellow as well as a true pioneer'.[1] During his flight Ham experienced seven minutes of weightlessness, and he performed tasks that involved pulling levers in response to coloured lights. His reward for a correct lever pull was a banana pellet, his punishment for a mistake an electric shock sent through his feet. According to one website devoted to 'animal astronauts', after being recovered from the craft, 'Ham was in good spirits and posed for pictures with the sailors on the recovery ship.'[2] The image of Ham, still in his space-couch, being handed an apple remains possibly the most famous picture of this pioneer (see opposite). His smile was beamed around the world. Ham lived for more than twenty years after his flight, and has a gravestone in the International Space Hall of Fame in Alamogordo, New Mexico.

But of course, this tale of animal heroism needs to be countered with other facts about the mission. In the first place, Ham was not a true name, it was an acronym for Holloman Aero-Medical, the military institution where he had been trained alongside five other chimpanzees. He had orig-inally been called '#65'.[3] In this instance the animal was only by accident given the individual status that comes with a name. In reality, his name was an institutional stamp of approval. In addition, NASA reports of the mission make clear its purpose: it was undertaken to check 'the reliability of the system'. The mission 'by the second Mercury-Redstone (MR-2) flight, with a chimpanzee aboard, [was] a final check to man-rate the capsule and launch the vehicle'. In essence, Ham's flight was never really regarded as a true flight, it was merely a test-run. The first true flight did not take place until three months after Ham's mission, when a human, Alan Shepherd, was recorded as 'the first American to blast off from Cape Canaveral'.[4] Ham's name was not really a name, and this great American pioneer was clearly not really an American. He was merely a means by which a space mission could be 'man-rated'.

The reason I am interested in Ham here, though, is because of the image of the chimp. The smile, and the general 'loveability' of the animal represent possible misinterpretations of the flight. While the baring of teeth in humans may be construed as a gesture of friendliness or happi-ness, in other primates teeth-baring can be a gesture of aggression or even fear.[5] This reaction in Ham is not surprising. During his flight he experi-enced delay after delay on the launch-pad at Cape Canaveral; 137 seconds into the flight the liquid oxygen supplies he was receiving became depleted; he was scheduled to experience 4.9 minutes of weightlessness but the length of time was actually 6.6 minutes in total; and the capsule came down 42 miles off course in the ocean, and water entered before he was finally rescued some 100 minutes after landing. All these faults, NASA tells us, were corrected before Shepherd went up.

So what does the picture of Ham tell us about ourselves? Our desire to interpret the smile of the chimp as evidence of his enjoyment of the expe-rience of space travel reflects, perhaps, our willingness to dismiss in certain contexts some of the differences between humans and animals. Ham looks like he's smiling, happy to receive his reward of an apple, and that's as far as many readers want to go with their interpretation of the image. But if we refuse this anthropomorphism – literally, changing of an animal into a human – then Ham's 'smile' becomes much more of a challenge. The bravery of the chimpanzee is translated into something that reflects, perhaps, the terror that he felt.

This image of a pioneer of the space-race – the USA's answer to the Soviet Union's space-dog, Laika, who died in space in 1957 when her oxygen supply ran out – can be seen as a symbol of contemporary Western attitudes towards animals. We interpret him as 'smiling' because that interpretation makes us happier, although we know that it might not be a smile at all. The animal becomes what we want it to be, and a reading that challenges this interpretation is also a challenge to many of the assumptions we have about how we should live with animals.

This section of the book picks up some of the issues raised in the (mis)reading of the image of Ham: recognition, misrecognition, visibility, invisibility. It looks at some of the problems inherent in the ways in which we interpret animals in three main areas of our lives: in their role as our pets, our food and our clothing. In one area – pet ownership – the animal is identified, given a name and a status, whereas in the others – food and clothing – the individual animal disappears and what appears in its place is a cellophane-wrapped lump of unidentifiable pink flesh or a coat. The question of why and how we manage this move from visible to invisible in our relationship with animals is one focus here; the other is what a reversal of the shift might achieve.

Puppy Love

Is a pet an animal? This might sound like a rather odd question, but it is one that is worth asking. A pet, simply put, is an animal who enters our (human) domestic space. It is different from other – non-tame or wild – animals, because it lives with us in our homes. On this basis, it is possible to see pets as making up a different class of creature. They are both human and animal; they live with us, but are not us; they have names like us, but cannot call us by our names.

Historically, while pets were presents in ancient Greek and Roman culture,[6] widespread ownership of animals with, as the legal definition would have it, no utilitarian function, emerges as a category during the sixteenth century, a time when domestic livestock – cows, pigs – were being removed from the home. Where, in the Middle Ages, humans and domestic animals shared their living quarters in the 'long house', as the medieval becomes the early modern world, domestic animals are removed from the shared home and given their own shelter.[7] And, where one animal – the domestic (and therefore edible) – is removed from close contact with humans, so, another – individualized (and therefore inedible) – enters. This happens at the same time as homes gain windows, and as bedrooms built separate from other living areas begin to appear in the most basic houses.[8] Increased privacy – a new human individuality – occurs at the moment when the increased individualism of the pet is also being established.

This individualization of animals was not always greeted with such ease as it is now. In sixteenth and seventeenth-century thought a pet was sometimes understood to upset the boundary between human and animal. For Edward Topsell, writing in 1607, the lap-dog, that epitome of the lady-like pet, represented women's inferiority. He wrote that 'these dogs are little, pretty, proper and fine, and sought for to satisfy the delicateness of dainty dames and wanton women's wills . . . [They are] instruments of folly for them to play and dally withal, to trifle away the treasure of time, to withdraw their minds from more commendable exercises, and to content their corrupted concupiscences with vain disport.' The relationship between the woman and her lap-dog was regarded as dangerously maternal, and even, perhaps, dangerously erotic:

These puppies the smaller they be, the more pleasure they provoke, as more meet play-fellows for mincing mistresses to bear in their bosoms, to keep company withal in their chambers, to succour in their bed, and nourish with meat at board, to lay in their laps, and lick their lips as they ride in their wagons.[9]

The pet, in this instance, provokes a fear about boundaries: neither fully animal, and therefore properly outside of the bed, nor fully human, and therefore properly inside, the lap-dog represents a 'grey area', the probing of which produces fears about the status of both pet and owner.

But, however it was figured, the change in the living relation with animals did not give a legal status to the pet. At the end of the sixteenth century, the jurist William Lambard argued that if an animal was 'for pleasure only', that is, if it did not serve a practical function like a horse or a cow, then it was 'not of any value', and to steal it was no crime.[10] What this legal refusal to recognize the significant emotional function of pets shows is that the kind of links between humans and animals that we take for granted now have not always been so commonsensical; that with the emergence of pet keeping came the emergence of other ideas – legal, moral, emotional – that created the modes of thought in place in the early twenty-first century. It was not until the nineteenth century, for example, that pets were given legal status, but even now that status is as property, and gradations of value are still in place. According to the 1972 Road Traffic Act, for example, a driver must stop and report an accident that involves injury to a dog, but the Act does not recognize the cat. Running over a cat is something that requires no report, although, as Noël Sweeney has noted, the driver can be prosecuted under the 1911 Protection of Animals Act, for causing the animal 'unnecessary suffering'.[11]

The gap between dog and cat, between legal subject and the disenfranchised moggy was, however, upset in 1994. As Peter Hillmore records, police in Bexleyheath arrested a dog for killing a cat. 'If this attack had been on a child,' said a police spokesperson, 'there would have been uproar, but because it's a cat nobody cares much, but we think it is a serious matter.' The police applied the law of 'deodand', in which an animal could be considered to have caused damage or death, for which – and this is the crucial point – the (human) owner of the animal was regarded as responsible. An animal is not considered to be 'guilty' in itself, because guilt implies intent, something that an animal, an irrational subject before the law, is incapable of.[12] But the law of deodand would appear to give an animal a (limited) active presence in the law. This is something that is, however, questioned by the facts of another case in Hillmore's article. Set side by side, the two cases show the truly ambivalent legal representation of animals. Hillmore tells the sad story of PC Steve Hansom, who was 'called out in Sunderland after a fight had broken out when a man accused his neighbour of teasing the pet tabby Tiddles. Constable Hansom sorted out the row, got into his car – and promptly ran over Tiddles.' Hillmore notes, with some pleasure it must be said, 'there wasn't even an inquest, PC Hansom was not suspended and his crime was not likened to the running over of a child'.[13] To say that there is confusion in the law as it represents pets is to understate the importance of an animal's simultaneous status as subject with legal rights and object with none at all.

But whatever confusions the law may throw up with relation to the status of pets, it is somehow separate from the domestic sphere in which the pet lives. The fact that a pet cat can be run over and the accident legally be left unreported really doesn't impinge on our emotional tie to the creature during its life. Most of us may not have realized that some areas of the law represent dogs differently from cats, and we don't cease to care for cats once we do recognize it. What is important though is the continuing confusion. The separateness of the law from our lived relation to our pets is once again made clear in another historical narrative that shows more directly how the status of the pet has changed across time, and with it, how relations to the pet have also changed. Once again it is the boundary between subject and object, human and animal, that is upset.

Keith Thomas has argued that it is not until the eighteenth century that pets were conventionally given human names, as opposed to specifically doggy names – like Rover; or catty names – like Puss.[14] In Shakespeare's *The Two Gentlemen of Verona*, written about 1593, for example, Lance, the servant of one of the eponymous gentlemen, has 'the sourest-natured dog that lives'; it is called Crab.[15] At the beginning of the nineteenth century, however, the utilitarian philosopher Jeremy Bentham owned a cat, first called Sir John Langborn, and then, as it got older, renamed the Reverend John Langborn, and finally the Reverend Doctor John Langborn.[16] In contemporary Western culture we have moved even further than this giving of human names and fictional qualifications to the animal: the dog-wedding still raises eyebrows, but it is a kind of logical development in the history of pets. Giving a dog a name is giving a dog the status of an individual, and individuals often form life partnerships. Giving pets a limited legal status might imply that other laws should also be in place for them; therefore, what is to say that Harold the spaniel might not wish to spend the rest of his life in a legally binding contract with Milly the setter?

The changes in the place of animals in our domestic life show us a new understanding of our relation to the non-human in the home. As one report of a dog-wedding noted: 'There are 61 million pet-owning households [in the USA] and many of them consider their pets part of the family.'[17] For this reason, companies supplying the needs of pet owners are burgeoning. The dog-wedding is becoming big business. A quick search of the Internet reveals a number of companies – Pooch Palace, Pawtytime – specializing in dog-related merchandise, and the wedding outfit – for the bride and groom – is a fixture of these sites. A dog wedding dress (available in ivory or white) costs around $60. Other outfits are also available: a prayer shawl and cap for the Jewish dog; a Superman outfit for the heroic pet. What businesses like this show is that many pet owners must have substantial disposable incomes; what they also show is that we no longer worry in the same way about the boundaries between human and pet that were drawn in the seventeenth century. As the article on the dog-wedding goes on to note: 'In a recent lawsuit, a California judge was asked to consider not just who has the legal title to one of the dogs in a divorce case, but where the dog would be better off.' The author continues, 'A growing movement is asking courts to abandon centuries of precedent and treat pets not as property or livestock, but something similar to humans.'[18]

This is the reason that, to return to my earlier point, I ask whether a pet is really an animal. There is a particularity in our relationship with them; where our relationships with a pet may be the closest contact many of us have with non-humans, that does not mean that we can take the pet as a simple representation of all animals. As Marc Shell has argued, loving a pet does not necessarily produce a more general love of animals. Rather, the pet can be – and usually is – loved as an individual creature, distinct from notions of species or any other category.[19] A pet is a pet first, an animal second.

But this, of course, does not mean that the relationship with the pet is not worthy of examination. Even if we accept that the pet can never be used to speak of our relationships with other (non-pet) animals, there is still something in our intimacy with them that raises a number of issues about how we, humans, currently understand the world around us. Marjorie Garber has argued that the close bonds we form with animals have many positive benefits for humans: for one thing, she argues, they 'humanize' us. That is, paradoxically, 'care, affection and even institutions directed at animals' make us more human.[20] This modern attitude again highlights the changes that have taken place in the last four centuries. In the late sixteenth and early seventeenth centuries pet ownership was regarded as potentially dehumanizing: the owner could be associated with bestiality. Now owning a pet enhances our status as humans.

But the humanizing qualities of the pet that are central to contemporary understanding can be seen in other areas than this. Garber also relates research at the State University at Buffalo Medical School that suggested that a dog is better at calming a stressed owner than is a spouse. Garber's reading of this is an important one: she writes, 'Most dog owners can guess the reason why: dogs never judge us and never compete with us.'[21] The pet is a reassuring presence as it can never speak back, can never disagree, or if it does, can easily be punished. But Garber's reading of the beneficial impact of the pet returns us to the image of Ham the chimpanzee 'smiling' on his return from space. We interpret the smile as a sign of happiness – he's pleased to have his feet firmly on solid ground again – and ignore, or refuse to countenance, the possibility that the smile might tell us something else; something that might undermine the way we are using this animal. Similarly, the pet's refusal to judge its owner is not, of course, a refusal, but a breakdown in communication. If a dog is judging its owner, how could the owner ever know? The only interpretation available to us is to assume that the dog has a position like that of a spouse or child, and that it has chosen not to judge; it has chosen to agree, even in its silence. This is what makes the dog (or any other pet for that matter) such a comfort. We can put thoughts into the pet's head – 'see how he loves me', we say to ourselves with satisfaction – but these are always thoughts we want the pet to have. Other humans have the unfortunate habit of voicing their own opinions, and sometimes these are opinions that we do not want to hear.

It is here once again that the pet crosses over species boundaries. It is an animal – it cannot speak – but it is also an ideal human – it says what we want it to say. It is only when the pet displays its animal nature – when it pees on the carpet, brings in a half-dead sparrow, destroys the furniture – that we lose the tranquillity of the relation. Then, and only then, do we really confront the existence of something beyond our control in our home. If a child peed on the carpet, a system of potty-training might be put in place, and it would be hoped that ultimately the child would recognize the urge to urinate, and learn to go to the toilet. Similarly, a pet can be house-trained, with the ultimate hope that it would learn to go out, or use the litter tray when necessary. However, if a child destroys furniture (I recall using a felt-tip pen to cause damage as a child) he or she might get 'a good talking to'. A pet, however, cannot be spoken to on the same terms (which is not to say that we don't try). Punishment might come, instead, in the form of a smack, or being shut outside, both actions that would be inappropriate (not to say illegal) ways of punishing a child. There is a repeated ambivalence here. Both like us and not like us, the pet once again escapes categorization beyond that of being a pet.

Another, larger, ambivalence emerges, however, when the question of edibility comes into play. Marc Shell argues that where structuralist anthropologists identified the significance of the 'incest taboo' in human cultures (the cultural restriction on sexual partners that disallows sexual relationships within the family – endogamy, and promotes relationships outside – exogamy), so in pet ownership we can see what might be termed a 'cannibalism taboo'.[22] That is, there is a restriction on what can be eaten that is based on similar ideas of inside and outside the family. We can eat a cow but cannot eat a cat. The distinction is not made on the basis of taste – in that, for example, cat flesh is horrible – but on the basis of closeness. What appears natural – that certain animals appear on menus and others don't – may actually be based upon some more deep-seated understanding of how we live with animals. And this is where we can begin to think about one of the many paradoxes of our current relations with animals: my initial figure here is the rabbit, but ultimately the rabbit will allow us to think about animals and edibility more generally.

Rabbit Pie and Eyelashes

As a child my mother fed me rabbit pie, but called it by the pseudonym 'chicken pie'. The reason she did this is simple. For me, the rabbit was an animal to be petted, not potted, and her deception was meant to protect my sensibilities. The fact that I couldn't bear the idea of eating rabbit speaks of an inability to draw a line between what is pet and what is food, an inability that I would, I think it was assumed, grow out of. I did. Now, as a vegetarian, I know where to draw the line between edibility and inedibility: my boundary is clear, it excludes all animals. As a rabbit lover, however, the boundary was decidedly unclear; somehow a confusion between petting and eating had entered the debate and the idea of eating what was perceived to be a pet would have been unthinkable. But, with hindsight, the discomfort over this uncertainty was felt most strongly, perhaps, by my parents, the knowing rabbit eaters (I, after all, remained in ignorant bliss). The discomfort that they perceived in me might actually have been their own discomfort, and the retitling of the pie's contents for their benefit as much as for my own. It is not only that I was confused, but that in my confusion I had, perhaps, signalled a confusion for my parents. My recognition forced my mother's own recognition that eating rabbit was somehow problematic, and the renaming took place. Sigmund Freud proposed that the 'jest' allows for 'the silencing [of] the objections raised by criticism which would not allow for the pleasurable feeling to emerge'.[23] In this instance the objections that might have emerged from me, the rabbit lover, were silenced through the adult use of a code (for 'rabbit' read 'chicken', the code-breaker would note), and the enjoyment of the rabbit pie could continue because of the 'protection' of the feelings of the rabbit eaters themselves.

But, of course, the rabbit lover's inability to draw a clear line between pet and pot is the more logical response than the rabbit eater's. Many of us are appalled at the idea that in some areas of the world dog is eaten. In the UK most of us are – to bring it closer to home – horrified at the idea of eating horse: and the French delicacy, frogs' legs, has become a shorthand for a national stereotype. But the dual function of the rabbit is one that we manage to live with. We know that there is a difference between the rabbit that roams the countryside, and the one that lives in a hutch in the back garden, and yet somehow the idea of eating rabbit can for some undercut the naturalized ways in which we eat meat: that is, it can remind us that what lies behind the Sunday roast is a real, living, breathing animal.

In her book *The Sexual Politics of Meat* Carol Adams argues that in meat-eating the animal is made into the 'absent referent': that is, that the flesh that is served up at the table is not perceived to be related to the animal that moves about in the field. When meat is purchased it often comes plastic-wrapped, boned, sliced. It doesn't look like its origin. In this way, we can eat beef burgers without thinking about cows; or sausages without thinking about pigs. Somehow the animalness of the meat is lost, and, for Adams, this is what must be countered if we are to challenge the naturalized power of the human that is revealed at the meal table. We must be made aware of the anthropocentrism that is exercised when we bite into a hamburger. Adams argues that in the process of eating 'we re-position the animal from subject to object by making ourselves the subjects in meat-eating'.[24] The pig is no longer an individual, a subject, it is an object; a chop, a rasher, a slice, a steak.

In English the linguistic difference between many animals and the meat they are transformed into aids this omission of the animal from the act of eating. We don't eat cows, we eat beef; for sheep there is mutton; for pigs pork. This linguistic distinction has its historical origin in the Norman invasion, when those who tended the (living) animals were Saxons, and used the English terms for the animals: cow, sheep, pig. The consumers of the animals, on the other hand – the Normans – used French terms that entered into the English language, and which in their original form relate to both the animal and its meat product: in French *boeuf* means both cow and beef; *mouton* both mutton and sheep; *porc* both pork and pig. It is the French terms that have become anglicized for the description of meat. But, what has happened since then is that these terms have lost their historical reference and reinforce the absence of the animal at the meal table. So much has this been naturalized that we can sit with a pet by the table – feeding it titbits – without recognizing any kind of paradox. A dog is not for eating, whereas pork can be eaten without us even recognizing the pig from which it came. This is the secret of the dinner table. And when there is a bringing together of the animal species and the meat – as in the eating of lamb – somehow the transfer of the term between living animal and chop ceases to be a problem: even here it is naturalized, and the lamb on the plate is distinguished from the lamb in the field.

The rabbit, though, for the urban meat-eater particularly, presents different problems from the lamb. The lamb exists outside the home: it is not usually a pet. The rabbit, however, can be a pet, and it is this figuring of the creature as simultaneously inside and outside that creates the problem. If a pet is a member of the family, and you have grown up with rabbits as pets, then eating a rabbit is not wholly different from eating your sister. When a pig was kept in the backyard, as Robert Malcolmson and Stephanos Mastoris have shown, it was always-already a food source.[25] Even as it was looked after, almost petted, its end was always firmly in sight. A pet rabbit is never food, and because of this the rabbit sits somewhere between two classes of animal: the pet and the edible. It is in our homes as companion, but it is also in our homes as pie-filling. *Lapin*, the French term for rabbit, has not entered the English language to help build a linguistic barrier. This is perhaps why there is something potentially troubling about the idea of eating rabbit, and it is perhaps for this reason that my mother called rabbit chicken.

But, there is another reason why a chicken is unquestionably edible and a rabbit only problematically so: rabbits are cute. This might sound like a crass way of thinking about the complex boundaries that we have built between ourselves and animals, and between different groups of animals, but the cultural place of the animal does affect the ways in which we think about its status. This goes beyond merely confining the edible to a hunk of something pink (and often plastic-wrapped), it includes other ways in which we see animals, and represent them to ourselves.

Rabbits, for Roger A. Caras, have 'a very high cuddle-factor'. He goes on, 'the "bunny" we know today is the epitome of cute'.[26] These animals have entered our mythology – through children's books, fables, films – as possessing qualities that transform them from being mere animal to potential individual. We recognize in the rabbit something more than just 'rabbit': there is, in the bunny, the image from Beatrix Potter books, childhood, the pet. But of course this picture of the rabbit as only problematically edible might fit certain areas of our societies, but elsewhere might signal important distinctions that need to be made between the urban and the rural. In the countryside hunting rabbits has two key functions. It can be a protection of crops, but also a source of cheap food. Here, the rabbit is rarely placed in an ambivalent position. A wild rabbit is, like a domestic pig, always potential food, and the more generally urban fears about the crossing over of the pet/food boundary are not traced. But it is not only the crossover between pet and meal that makes the relation to meat sometimes problematic. Where the idea of dominion supports, and possibly encourages, meat-eating, an alternative relation to animals – stewardship – can force us to rethink things. We can see this in the protests over the export of live veal calves that took place in England in 1995.

The production of veal is one of those processes usually kept behind closed doors. As consumers all we usually see is the pale flesh in restaurants and in supermarkets. The protests in early 1995, however, changed the way that veal was perceived as the modes of meat production were moved to centre-stage. A calf destined for the veal trade is, to use the industrial term, the 'by-product' of the dairy industry. Dairy cows are artificially inseminated, and give birth, for the primary purpose of producing of milk. Their calves do not always enter the dairy stock, and some of them – one estimate has the number at 400,000 a year from the UK – are exported to the continent to be raised in crates, and become, in death, veal.[27] Veal crates, the tiny boxes that house the calves, do not allow the calf to comfortably sit or turn, and were banned in the UK in 1990, but remain in use on the continent. It is for this reason that so many live British calves are exported. Just as the production of pâté de foie gras takes place by force-feeding geese grain that expands their livers, so veal is created when calves are fed an iron- and fibre-deficient diet for the six months or so that they live in the crate so that their flesh is pale. In veal production what is clear is that the end justifies the means: the public taste for veal vindicates the process that produces it. However, the protests at Brightlingsea in Essex, and Shoreham in East Sussex that gained the headlines defamiliarized this process: that is, they laid it bare for inspection. This reintroduced the animal into the equation and, just as Carol Adams had argued, once the animal was in view the attitude towards its edibility changed. News footage of the transporter lorries full of calves going over to veal crates on the continent broke down the separation of meat and animal: suddenly the meal had a face. The pale flesh belonged to something, it was no longer isolated from its origin.

But, it is the nature of the animal here that is, I think, particularly important. We are often willing to ignore meat production processes – we know, for example, that battery hens live (if that is the right word) in the most appalling conditions – but somehow the veal calves were different. One of the overwhelming factors in these protests was the sense that these were young, helpless animals ripped from their mothers. They were deserving not of our dominion, but of our stewardship. This makes sense of the fact that, as Ted Benton and Simon Redfearn have noted, many of the protesters were meat-eaters, and were not regular political activists. A sign in a Colchester pub read: 'You Don't Have to Stop Eating Meat to Care – Ban Live Exports.' This was a protest – for some – about the transportation methods, and, particularly, the treatment of calves, not the treatment of animals more generally. Benton and Redfearn note the glee with which one newspaper reported 'the irony of protesters taking a break from struggling with the police to hungrily consume hot bacon rolls'.[28] Just as a pet can represent a limited horizon in animal love, so the veal calf was, for some protesters, separated from more general debates about eating meat. In the same year as the protest, Gallup undertook a survey on behalf of *The Daily Telegraph*, and the results certainly record this limitation in our animal love: 11 per cent of respondents agreed with the statement that 'it is not right to slaughter cows, sheep and other animals for food,' while 68 per cent agreed with the statement 'it is not right to export veal calves to the continent.'[29]

So why calves? Just as the pet is neither human nor animal, but somewhere in between, so, in this instance, the calf was figured as neither animal (and therefore edible) nor human (and therefore able to look after itself). It was a young animal – calves are only a week old when they are transferred to the crates – and a young animal that, like a child, needed protection. The sight of weeping protesters, crying for the plight of the calves, reinforced the image of the veal calf as a kind of 'Bambi' figure. As with many cartoon animals, calves have big eyes and long eyelashes. We look into the eyes of the calf and see, not an alien species, but something dangerously recognizable. We see, in fact, a version of ourselves. Fish and chickens, for example, do not have big eyes and long eyelashes, and this is perhaps one reason that the battery farming of eggs is often protested against only by those who have a wider interest in animal welfare. On their own, chickens are not regarded as worthy of the kind of attention that the calves received. Fish are an even more extreme version of this: some fish-eaters, for example, regard themselves as vegetarians.

These two groups of animals – fish and chickens – also fall foul of what might be regarded as an older version of vegetarianism. Where contemporary vegetarianism is based, usually, on ethical questions, eighteenth-century vegetarianism was often about health concerns. George Cheyne, for example, argued in 1720 that an avoidance of animal flesh can 'Cure or effectively Relieve the Gout'.[30] The avoidance of animal flesh had nothing to do with the animal itself; the ethic, if you like, is missing. Likewise, in contemporary society, red meat is still regarded as more damaging in terms of cholesterol levels, and fish and chicken are regarded as healthy flesh. So these creatures fail on two counts: not only do they lack a certain recognizability, and so are distanced from their consumers, their flesh is also understood to be good for us. The two ideals support one another: one does not look into the eyes of a chicken and see oneself, therefore one can more easily eat a chicken, call it a healthy diet, and not be confronted with some of the moral questions that are brought into play when other animals are considered. In this sense, the calf exists somewhere between human and animal: it becomes, perhaps, a symbolic – and helpless – human, and in the export of live veal calves what was revealed was the hypocrisy of our construction of ourselves as 'a nation of animal lovers'.

This phrase emerged once again in the recent outbreak of foot-and-mouth disease. And it should come as no surprise that it was in relation to a calf that the British people showed their 'generosity' towards the so-called lower animals. After two months of the outbreak and nearly 1,500 cases of the disease, a calf was discovered alive after spending five days under a pile of fifteen healthy but slaughtered cattle (one of which was its mother). Because of the culling policy then in place, which stated that all animals on farms 'contiguous' to suspected outbreaks should also be slaughtered to stop the spread of the disease, Phoenix, as the calf was appropriately named, despite her astonishing survival of the first cull on her farm in Devon, was due to be put to death. The media, however, intervened, and this thirteen-day-old white calf came to symbolize the unrest at the mass slaughter of animals that was taking place. *The Daily Mirror* received numerous letters from readers about the plight of Phoenix, and the sentiments in many of the letters echo some of the ideas already outlined in this chapter: 'My God! My God!' wrote one correspondent, 'Please, Please, I beg you. Don't kill this beautiful calf. He [*sic*] hasn't got a voice, we have.' Another, this time a petition, read, 'Don't kill me like you killed my mother.'[31] The anonymity of the slaughter of cattle was disrupted by a calf with a name. Suddenly what was absent – the individual – became overwhelmingly and powerfully present.

The officials of the Ministry of Agriculture (MAFF) seemed to miss this point, and suggested that the public response to the fate of Phoenix was one of 'hideous sentimentality'. But, with a General Election on the horizon, Tony Blair perhaps recognized the political possibilities of the case of the innocent (white) calf. As the pro-Labour *Mirror* reported it, the Prime Minister 'personally stepped in to reprieve Phoenix and show that he was listening to the nation'. The report goes on, 'If Phoenix had been killed, her death would have haunted the Prime Minister.'[32] As a nation of animal lovers (and at this stage it is worth reminding ourselves that over two million animals had been culled) issues about the economy, asylum seekers, public services were dwarfed by the tiny calf. The Prime Minister, so adept at working the popular press, used this calf as a way of presenting himself not as a politician who may have failed the farming community, but as a politician proud to see the popular interest in this one calf reflecting his own deeply held feelings towards animals. (This was, of course, something that Downing Street later denied, as it would cast a shadow over the seriousness of the agricultural policy decision that was made when MAFF stopped the cull of animals on contiguous farms.)

The shift from being an anonymous product of the agriculture industry to a media celebrity with a name and a history also forced a shift in Phoenix's future. Michaela Broad, her owner, stated: 'Phoenix is now going to grow up and is going to be company for our pony Teddy. She is going to have as much grass as she can eat and going to have a good life.'[33] From meat to pet, object to subject, Phoenix's journey is just one well-documented illustration of the paradoxical ways in which we live with animals. Even as millions of healthy animals are sent to be slaughtered we are able to celebrate the fact that we truly are 'a nation of animal lovers'.

The producers of meat and dairy goods know that this is how we wish to position ourselves, and reflect our desire in their promotions. Anchor, for example, make clear that the cattle that provide the milk for their butter live 'naturally'. On their website the response to the question 'Why is butter yellow?' gives room for a simple form of advertising.

> Actually, not all butter is yellow. In many countries where cows are fed on grain, butter is very pale, like cream. But because New Zealand cows are fed on grass, their milk contains a yellow/orange pigment called beta-carotene which makes our butter yellow (and gives it more Vitamin A, which is important for good vision).[34]

The implication of this, of course, is that, as the television adverts emphasize, these are 'free range cows'. That is, unlike the cattle used by other butter manufacturers who are fed grain (which is, it is inferred, I think, not natural), Anchor's cattle are, apparently, free to roam the lush hills of New Zealand, with the obvious implication that these cows, despite being the fodder of the food industry, have good lives. This representation of the process of production as being a part of the natural life of the animal, of course shields the consumer from the other version of events that the veal calf protests made clear, and here, even when the animal is made visible, it is an acceptable visibility.

This recognition that, even in some of the most extreme moments, when meat and animal are linked, meat-eating as a whole is not brought under question was also made evident in the BSE crisis. When links between 'mad cow disease' and Creuzfeld-Jakob disease (CJD) in humans were traced, a panic emerged about eating beef. The fact that the meat-production industry had (often unknowingly) been feeding cows, naturally herbivorous animals, not merely feed made from animal remains, but remains from their own species, was somehow secondary to the panic about human health that ensued. And the outcome was not a challenge to meat-eating on a large scale, but an avoidance of beef; other meats emerged to replace what was deemed to be no longer edible.

Somehow meat-eating is now so firmly a part of Western culture that even potential health risks cannot begin to question the naturalization of the consumption of animal flesh.

This sense that meat-eating now holds a naturalized position in Western culture can also be traced in another way. The defamiliarization of meat – the linking of the meat to the animal that it comes from – has actually become part of the process of eating meat. What has emerged is a kind of celebration of meat-eating that exists, perhaps, because of the threat to the naturalness of it that has been mounted by the various vegetarian and environmental groups that now hold some power within the food industry. Just as we might see the emergence of the 'new lad' as a reaction against the acceptance of certain feminist ideals, so, perhaps, the anxiety that can be traced in some areas of meat-eating culture might also be linked to the growing acceptance of vegetarianism: in the late 1990s, for example, 7 per cent of the population over fifteen years old classed themselves as vegetarian, and in 1996 '25 per cent of non-vegetarians considered that their children were likely to become vegetarian'.[35] By implication, the next generation of parents will be eating less and less meat, as, it can be assumed, will their children. As a defence against this growing move towards vegetarianism, the fact that meat-eating is the eating of an animal has to be advertised, to be lionized.

The recent advertisements for 'Peperami', the spicy meat sausage, celebrate the origin of the snack. 'Peperami,' one advert says, 'it's a bit of an animal.' The animated figure of the 'Peperami' sausage has its own dedicated website and merchandise, and is a celebration of all things anarchic.[36] The voice of the sausage in the adverts is Ade Edmondson's, the creator of arch-anarchist Vyvian in the 1980s TV series *The Young Ones*. The sausage is a new lad: a self-proclaimed animal. This representation of the meat product as animal undercuts Carol Adams's argument that visibility would disturb the practice of meat-eating, and works at the opposite extreme. To eat a Peperami is to engage in the process that defines the superiority of humanity; is to celebrate anthropocentrism.

The meat-eater's fearfulness that I am tracing in this advertising campaign can also be found in another place. Anti-animal rights websites, for example, are emerging, where details of materials that will bolster this 'philosophical' position can be found. One such site points its viewer to *The Detroit News* of 2 May 1998, and Jeffrey Alan Ford's article 'Appreciate Animals to Pieces with a Fork and Knife.' Ford's argument is crude in its simplicity, but gives a clear sense that the life of the carnivore is a threatened one. He writes; 'I love animals to pieces – square-shaped bite-size pieces that can be served medium-rare next to my oven-baked potato and crispy dinner salad.' He continues in the same vein:

> that's not to say I don't appreciate animals for purposes other than the fulfillment of my ravenous appetite. I also believe they make beautiful clothing and provide excellent contributions to our health and well-being when they are the subject of rigorous and extensive testing in the world's finest clinical laboratories.[37]

Somehow, all the apparent progress that has been made since the first animal welfare campaigns began in earnest in the early nineteenth century seems to have been left behind,[38] and a new position, not 'new laddism' but 'new anthropocentrism', has emerged. And the reason is clear: Ford writes of the 'pity' he feels for 'poor vegetarians' whose lack of certain proteins, available from meat alone, might, he writes, 'cause so many of the animal rights wackos to place the relatively inconsequential lives of furry little critters ahead of the lives of their fellow humans'.[39] This is a typical and simplistic formulation: of course vegetarianism does not equate to misanthropy, and Adolf Hitler is not the archetypal vegetarian. But statements such as Ford's represent the growing impact that the move against meat-eating is having. If vegetarianism were not becoming so widespread, or even such an accepted part of our cultures in the twenty-first century, why would this meat-eater be so fearful? Somehow, at the bottom of the new anthropocentrism lies the fear of anti-anthropocentrism; the growing recognition that animals may well be worthy of more than they are being allowed at the moment. Perhaps animal rights campaigns have been more successful than might be thought. Like the pseudonymous chicken pie, there is a recognition that questioning what we do with animals is something that we know needs to happen, but is, at the same time, something that we resist, repress, because the outcomes of such a questioning might be too far-reaching. Animals live in our natural world, and I mean that in two ways. Animals are a part of the natural world – (non-pet) animals exist 'out there', beyond human control. But at the same time the ways in which we use animals have come to be natural. To recognize that what we are now assuming are ideas that are, at heart, deeply contradictory, may force us to look for an alternative relation. But that alternative relation might force us to rethink more than just what we put on our plates; it might challenge a whole world view, and that is something we shy away from.

Any philosophical position that wishes to support a relocation of our relationship with animals has to counter the ways in which anthropocentrism has been naturalized; it has to look again at the ways in which we segregate the animal community into different categories – edible, inedible; pet, wild; cute, ugly. This is, I think, one of the most powerful aspects of the work of one philosopher of animal rights: Peter Singer.

The Philosophical Animal

Singer's *Animal Liberation* was first published in 1975, and placed the question of the ways in which we use animals – in laboratories, agriculture, food – firmly in the domain of philosophy. As Singer himself notes in his Preface to the 1990 edition of the book, 'The liberation movements of the Sixties had made Animal Liberation an obvious next step.'[40] The dominion of

Western culture had already been attacked as patriarchal, racist, homophobic, and now it was regarded as 'speciesist'. This term, now included in the *OED*, was coined by Richard Ryder in the same year as the publication of Singer's book, and represents 'the widespread discrimination that is practised by man against other species'. Ryder aligns speciesism explicitly with racism and argues that 'speciesism and racism are both forms of prejudice that are based upon appearances – if the other individual looks different then he is rated as being beyond the moral pale'. By announcing a link between the civil rights movement and the animal liberation movement, Ryder had found a political tool for working against the naturalized dominion that persists in our relationship with animals. 'Racism,' he writes, 'is condemned today by most intelligent and compassionate people and it seems only logical that such people should extend their concern for other races to other species also.'[41] Claiming a philosophical and historical precedent for the movement was vital.

Singer's work operates within a similar discourse of logic. He recognizes the important parallel to the late eighteenth century, when Tom Paine's *Rights of Man* was extended by Mary Wollstonecraft in her *Vindication of the Rights of Woman*, which itself was finally (and comically) responded to by Thomas Taylor in his *Vindication of the Rights of Brutes*. In the twentieth century the question of liberation had been raised in different terms, but addressed the oppression of similarly marginalized groups: by the civil rights movement, the feminist movement and the gay liberation movement. This time, however, the addition of animals was no longer comic. It was wholly serious.

Singer attacked head-on some of our most embedded assumptions about the way we treat animals. One of his more infamous suggestions opens up one of the most important interventions that his work has made: it has denaturalized the ways we think about them. If, Singer argues, we agree that animals can feel pain then certain ways of living with animals need to be rethought in those terms, and one of the possible outcomes of this acknowledgement of a shared sentience would be a recognition that anticipation – for example the knowledge that one is to be experimented upon – might be the way of differentiating human from animal: an animal does not know it is to be used in this way, whereas an adult human would. This leads Singer to put forward the idea of experimentation on certain humans: 'this same argument gives us a reason for preferring to use human infants – orphans perhaps – or severely retarded human beings for experiments, rather than adults, since infants and retarded humans would also have no idea of what was going to happen to them'. What Singer is posing is a problem of logic. If we agree that animals can feel pain (which most of us, surely, do) then the reason for experimenting on animals, and not on humans becomes very difficult to find: one of the primary points of differentiation – the animal's lack of ability to anticipate the experiment – would also apply to some humans. Singer notes the logic of this: If we make a distinction between animals and [infants and retarded humans], on what basis can we do it, other than a bare-faced – and morally indefensible – preference for members of our own species?'[42]

The importance of this aspect of Singer's work is that it lays bare the kind of illogic at work in our relation with animals. By emphasizing that the logic we apply to animals can also be applied to some humans, Singer undercuts it, makes it untenable. Following this attack on one mode of thinking, Singer then applies an alternative theory to the ways in which we live with animals. He uses utilitarian arguments, which, put simply, propose that actions are wrong if they produce displeasure or unhappiness to the majority of those affected by them, and that, in contrast, ethical rightness can be assumed by an action producing the 'greatest happiness of the greatest number'. Taking up the question of the ways in which we treat animals, Singer moves beyond the illogic with which he begins his book, and uses some very basic arguments to counter certain anthropocentric assumptions.

Turning to meat production, Singer argues (and his figures were correct in 1990) that it takes 21 pounds of protein fed to a calf to produce one pound of animal protein (i.e. meat) for humans: 'we get back less than 5 per cent of what we put in'. Even a pig, where the ratio between food for the animal and meat produced is smaller, requires eight pounds of food for each pound of flesh. Most estimates, Singer argues, 'conclude that plant foods yield about ten times as much protein per acre as meat does', and the implication of this is that 'if Americans were to reduce their meat consumption by only 10 per cent for one year, it would free at least 12 million tons of grain for human consumption – or enough to feed 60 million people'. He goes on: 'Indeed, the food wasted by animal production in the affluent nations would be sufficient, if properly distributed, to end both hunger and malnutrition throughout the world.'[43] This is a huge claim, but it is a claim that is meant to move our eyes from what might be seen as a 'sentimental' attachment to animals – something that Jeffrey Alan Ford attacked – towards a more practical mode of thought. Eating animals is cruel (Singer spends a great deal of time outlining the cruelty involved in battery farming, veal production and so on), but it is also a foolish use of resources. What Singer does, then, is, in a variety of different ways, ask us to rethink certain assumptions about the ways we live with animals. Animals cannot be differentiated so clearly from humans, he argues, and using animals as sources of food is wasteful. Suddenly anthropocentrism is not natural, it is illogical, and it is foolish.

Singer's work has been criticized on a number of levels; in the popular media, the Animal Liberation Front (ALF) – often regarded as a group that gained its identity following the publication of Singer's seminal work – is represented as a terrorist organization. As Steve Baker has shown, even the RSPCA positioned itself, in one 1986 advert, as the antithesis of the ALF: 'Our supporters prefer to use a pair of scissors,' said the RSPCA ad (which included a form to cut out), beneath a picture of 'a furtive balaclava-clad figure shearing through a fence with a large pair of wire cutters'. Baker notes that, despite the two organizations' shared interest in animal welfare, 'it was almost as though these activists . . . were seen as a greater danger than those perpetrating animal cruelty and abuse'.[44] Singer's work, as it is taken up by a group like the ALF, is a million miles away from the ideas about animal welfare that many people, for example, took to the picket lines at Brightlingsea.

But criticism of Singer has also come from a very different place. Keith Tester has argued that what lies at the heart of the work by Singer, Tom Regan and other philosophers concerned with animal welfare is a paradoxical sense of the continuing centrality of the human. Tester writes: 'it would be interesting and not too deliberately polemical, to explore the hypothesis that animal rights is not concerned with animals at all; that, on the contrary, the idea says rather more about society and humans. Animal rights might really be about social actions and only incidentally focus on animals.' He goes on:

> Think for a moment about who asserts animals' rights. Is it a laboratory rabbit, veal calf, or hunted fox? Not at all. Animal rights is exclusively asserted by society and it is intended to restrain human practices. It says that animals are morally the same as humans, and then asks humans to treat them as if they were human; it is up to us to struggle for animal rights because animals cannot fight for themselves. In other words, they are different. Animal rights classifies animals as non-moral objects which are metonymical to moral (human) subjects, and as a metaphorical society which is morally relevant since human society is morally relevant. Society thinks about animals to think about itself.[45]

Ted Benton has proposed something similar: he argues that, because of the emphasis placed on likeness by animal rights philosophies – the fact that (most) animals share some traits, such as the ability to experience pain, with humans – 'the rights view certainly remains anthropocentric'.

Animals, he notes, are 'intrinsically incapable of exercising' rights; they must always have those rights 'given' to them by humans.[46]

Tester and Benton, however, differ significantly in the ways in which they develop their understanding of the problem of asserting animal rights. For Benton, the answer to this conundrum of the continuing anthropocentrism of animal rights philosophies is to propose something different: he argues that we should not think in terms of animals' rights (which would imply that the animal has certain responsibilities), but in terms of their needs. Tester, however, appears to abandon the possibility of ever thinking about animals without anthropocentrism. Moving on to look at ethological studies, he writes that animals are 'nothing other than what we make them. Society invests animals with moral significance and presses codes of normative behaviour. Society uses animals to understand itself.' Animals, he argues, are 'a blank paper'.[47] His argument is clearly a precursor of my own interpretation of the pet, the domesticated animal onto which we put meaning, but he does not limit this idea to the pet, and it is here, I think, that Tester's work becomes problematic. Where the pet might be interpreted as holding a specific position within the home, and therefore as holding a specific almost-human moral status, this moral status is gone when we think about all animals as only having the meaning that we give them. One of the implications of Tester's view is that there is no ethical space for animals, that there is only representational space – only what we make of animals – and this precludes any possibility of ethical intervention. If an animal really is only what we make it because we can only ever access that animal through human eyes, human language, human ideas, then, as Ted Benton has asked, 'perhaps, if we were to impose the socially produced category of fish upon the viper its bite would lose its venom?'[48] Somehow, Tester manages to close off even the possibility of thinking about animals in any other terms than anthropocentric ones.

I would like to dispute Tester's pessimistic stance, but can also see it at work in some of the ways we currently live with animals. Fake fur, I think, offers a vision of a world in which there are no real animals for us to live with, only human versions of animals. But fake fur also allows us to contemplate how we think with animals in the early twenty-first century.

Faking It

In 1994 the supermodel Naomi Campbell, along with four other models, posed naked for an anti-fur campaign launched by People for the Ethical Treatment of Animals (PETA). The campaign poster headline was 'We'd rather go naked than wear fur.' Three years later, Campbell was fired by PETA, and what followed was an acrimonious and public exchange between the model and the head of the organization. This tale of Campbell's troubled engagement with animal welfare offers a brief glimpse of some of the difficulties facing many consumers who wish to engage with both ethics and fashion in their daily lives. At the heart of Campbell's relationship with PETA are issues about style, freedom of choice, fakery and confusion. While Campbell has been labelled as a sell-out, it might be more productive to read the narrative of her rise and fall from grace as underlining issues that affect all consumers.

Central to Campbell's falling out with PETA was her role as a model, the very thing that made the organization interested in her in the first place. Having pledged to never wear or model fur in 1993, Campbell appeared in *W* magazine wearing real fur in 1996. At that time she claimed that she had been told that the fur she was modelling was fake, and PETA took her at her word. However, a year later in Milan, Campbell crossed the line between ethics and fashion when she took part in Karl Lagerfeld's catwalk show for Fendi, Italy's largest furrier. No excuses were available to Campbell, and she was fired by PETA's director of campaigns, Dan Matthews. His letter, widely quoted in the media, showed how appalled Matthews had been by Campbell's actions: 'Integrity may not mean much to you, but it does to us, so consider yourself fired . . . for reneging on your written promise never to model fur.'[49] From his perspective, Campbell's ethics were for sale to the highest bidder, and on this occasion, the fur industry won. But, as Carole White, the chief of Elite Premier, Campbell's modelling agency, said: 'This is all about the power of fashion.' She added, 'Quite a lot of the girls are back wearing real fur again.'[50] It may seem strange that at a time when animal welfare organizations and the causes they espoused were becoming more and more mainstream fur should re-enter the world of fashion. There are a number of ways of thinking about this, some of them more obvious, and less troubling than others. I will begin with the obvious and move to the troubling.

Fur has always been associated with two (interrelated) things: wealth and sexuality. Historically, sumptuary legislation made clear the link between fur and wealth. In an attempt to make class distinctions more apparent, laws were passed that limited what could be worn by whom. In the sixteenth century, cloth of gold, silver, satin, silk or sables could only be worn by earls and above; furs of black jennet were restricted to dukes, marquesses, earls, barons and knights; fur from animals found only outside the dominions of the monarch were to be worn only by men with an income of over £100 per year.[51] On this basis, fur was a clear designator of status. Only the wealthy could wear it. Portraits from the period often depict their subjects wearing fur, not only because it was fashionable, but because it was a shorthand representation of status. As Julia V. Emberley has noted, sumptuary legislation 'was meant not so much to curb extravagance as to preserve certain commodities for the wealthy, ensuring that symbolic displays of wealth were reserved to the property-owning classes'. She goes on to argue that the legislation may also have affected taste, may have increased the aesthetic value of fur. To wear the skin of a dead animal was, in fact, to place yourself within a small and exclusive community.[52]

Such symbolic qualities are still associated with fur. But the nature of the exclusivity of the community has, of course, changed. Fur is still associated with money, with an ostentatious display of wealth. It is also, for some, associated with glamour and sex. Furs.com, a website dedicated to fur fashions, saw 2000 as the year when fur returned to the world of glamour. Hollywood actresses, including Catherine Zeta-Jones, Cate Blanchett, Kate Hudson, and the female stars of *Friends* are all listed as having worn fur during the year. The website speaks of 'fashion [that] epitomized classic, movie star glamour reminiscent of classic Hollywood stars like Marilyn Monroe'. Fur, it argues, 'was key to getting the luxe, luscious look'. Having noted Naomi Campbell's return to fur, the article asked the question 'Does this mean that PETA's era of intimidation is over?'[53] Where, between 1985 and 1990 fur sales in Britain dropped by an estimated 75 per cent, from the evidence of recent catwalk shows, and the return of Hollywood to the old days of glamour, fur is making a return. An article in *The Independent* in 1996 spoke of 'a seemingly renewed acceptance of fur', noting that *Vogue* magazine for October of that year carried an advertisement for 'a Fendi fur-trim coat, while a headline in French Elle claims "It's OK to Wear Fur Again."'[54] Other fashion magazines, including *Marie Claire*, have anti-fur policies, but this is not the case for all. Alexandra Shulman, then editor of *Vogue*, was reported in 1997 as saying that *Vogue* had 'no hard and fast rules' on the inclusion of fur in editions of the magazine.[55] Content, it would appear, is dictated by the fashion industry.

This was all too evident on the catwalks of that year. Susannah Barron announced in *The Guardian* that fur was back: 'it wasn't just mink and fox that returned with a vengeance: there was a whole Noah's Ark out there, rounded up, slaughtered and made into clothes. Mongolian lamb, Persian lamb, snakeskin, ponyskin, feathers . . . surely some of this must be ethically unsound too?'[56] Where the fur industry will not only claim a long history – from the Stone Age and beyond – it will also, like the food industry, disguise, or at best not discuss, the source of the furs it uses. Much fur used in the fashion industry is farmed or ranched, that is, the fur-bearing animals are reared specially for use in clothing manufacture. But an unspecified amount of fur is also from the wild. It is often not possible to tell clearly where the fur that makes up a garment comes from, and with the closure of fur farms – in 1998 the British government announced its intention to outlaw fur farming, and close the remaining fifteen mink farms – it is likely that wild-animal skins are being used alongside ranched-animal skins. What also remains unstated is the number of skins that are needed to make up a single garment. In 1984 Lynx, the anti-fur charity, issued an advertisement with the by-line 'It takes up to 40 dumb animals to make a fur coat. But only one to wear it.' More recently, the California-based animal rights organization, Animal Emancipation, suggested that it takes 45 mink to make one coat.[57] This shows clearly that, like Peter Singer's figures on protein yield in the meat industry, our appetite for animals in the fashion industry is a voracious one.

More worrying, perhaps, than this link between fur, wealth, sexuality and commerce is the place of ethics in fashion. This is not only an issue to be raised by fashion houses – Stella McCartney famously refuses to use leather as well as fur. It is also an issue that we, as consumers, face every day. We can return to Naomi Campbell here, and to another issue that emerged from her spat with PETA. In an interview in *The Daily Telegraph* in 1997 Campbell raised a problem faced by many consumers: discussing her public separation from PETA she stated 'I eat meat, I wear leather; I don't want to be a hypocrite.'[58] The leather used for most shoes is a by-product of the meat industry. The skin of a slaughtered animal, according to Susanna Barron, can count for '10 per cent of its value in the abattoir'. Barron also notes that 'the softest, most desirable leather comes from unborn animals'.[59] With this link between the meat and fashion industries so clear in terms of leather, it does, as Campbell notes, seem hypocritical to refuse one product – fur – while continuing to use another – leather (and, Peter Singer and others would add, dairy products – milk, cheese and so on – are also by-products of the meat industry, so the only truly ethical diet is a vegan one). Fur, however, has always been placed in a separate position. For Mark Glover of Respect for Animals, fur 'represents the most extreme form of cruelty'.[60] It is categorically different from both meat and leather, in that it is absolutely unnecessary, ornamental in a way that meat and leather are not (although, of course, many would want to say that the latter two animal products are also always unnecessary). Wearing fur in the West is not the only way of keeping out the cold even though it serves this function. It is much more than that: it is a status symbol.

In other cultures, however, fur plays a different role, and the disjuncture between the West and cultures such as the Innuit and Dene in Canada have upset many simple ethical desires to ban fur. Emberley notes that the Greenpeace anti-sealing campaign of the 1980s led to a sharp fall in the price of sealskin: from $30 to $2 or $3 per skin. The impact of this plummet in prices upon the aboriginal communities was massive: defender of the fur trade, Hugh Brody has termed anti-fur organizations 'a new example of southern imperialist intrusion'.[61] Here we are not looking at fur as a merely ornamental addition to the wardrobe, it is a mainstay of the economy, and the desire to respect animals results in what could be regarded as a disrespect for the traditional ways of life of aboriginal peoples. How to bridge this divide between Western ethics and aboriginal practices, between animal welfare and indigenous survival remains a question almost impossible to answer. A claim can be made for the rights of aboriginal communities to continue their traditional relationship with the natural world. What must be acknowledged here, though, is that these traditions are not separate from commerce, but are inextricably linked. An animal killed for its fur by an Innuit trapper may become a coat worn on the catwalks of Milan. For the Innuit, fur is a business as well as a tradition, and for animal rights philosopher Tom Regan, this is the crux of the matter. He writes, 'Like anyone else who enters the world of business, those whose business it is to kill wild animals must understand that they waive their right not to be made worse-off if their business fails. We have no duty to buy their products, and they have no right to require that we keep either their business or their present quality of life afloat.'[62] But what if that business is claimed as a traditional way of living? What if, as Hugh Brody argued, anti-fur campaigns are another form of colonialism, just another way of wiping out alternative ways of living? Regan does not address this issue, and it is a gap in his argument. If we do not account for the key difference between, say, Fendi and the Innuit people (despite the fact that there may be commercial links between them), there is the possibility that we treat other cultures as if they were merely aberrant versions of ourselves, and 'discipline' them as such.

An unsatisfactory alternative solution to this conundrum might be that we leave the question, to wear or not to wear fur, up to the individual, and accept difference as an inevitability of late capitalism. I may have decided against wearing fur, the argument might go, but that does not mean that your decision to wear fur is a poor one. What needs to be remembered in the movement against fur, and the attack upon traditional trapping communities, is that the West can by no means regard itself as the source of ethics. Not only can the Christian religion be interpreted as supporting and promoting dominion and the practices that arise from it, it is in the developed world particularly that we find battery farms, veal crates, intensive farming techniques. On this basis Naomi Campbell's recognition of her potential hypocrisy is a true reflection of some of what is unsaid in debates about fur. Few of us can speak from a truly 'pure' position.

In the meantime, a compromise of strange proportions seems to have emerged: fake fur. Caught somewhere between fashion and ethics – the desire for the symbolic power of fur, but the refusal of the death of the animal – fake fur has emerged as a (cheaper) alternative to real fur. It might seem that with this nylon we can continue to celebrate our status as we simultaneously care about the natural world: have our cow and eat it, if you like. Fake fur has many of the connotations of real fur – luxury, sexuality –

without the pain. For the West this would seem to be an ideal way forward. We don't need to turn our backs on the fashion industry, but we can continue to live as partners rather than masters of animals.

If only it was as simple as this. Leaving aside the conundrum of the relationship between anti-fur campaigns and the destruction of aboriginal traditions (for which I have no solution), fake fur opens up the place of animals in human cultures in a profound and troubling way. In fact, fake fur, I want to argue, is truly postmodern. That is, it is an object that seems to take up some of the ideas that have emerged in philosophy in the last three decades, and to present some of the same problems that those ideas bring with them. A brief outline of some key debates from one area of postmodern thought might help to explain this.

In 1981 the philosopher Jean Baudrillard argued that the world is made up, not of our experience of 'the real', but of 'simulations' of the real. He writes, 'It is no longer a question of imitation, nor of reduplication, nor even of parody. It is rather a question of substituting signs of the real for the real itself . . . Never again will the real have to be produced.' For Baudrillard, Disneyland is 'a perfect model' of what he regards as 'the entangled orders of simulation'. He goes on, 'Disneyland is presented as imaginary in order to make us believe that the rest is real, when in fact all of Los Angeles and the America surrounding it are no longer real, but of the order of the hyperreal and of simulation.' That is, in Disneyland we think we are getting a knowingly fake representation of the real world – in which mice talk and fairies exist – whereas, according to Baudrillard, what we are really getting is evidence of the absence of the real more generally.[63] The real, what exists outside of Disneyland, is itself a simulation, and the fake is just a simulation of a simulation. There is no 'real' America out there, only the hyperreal. Disneyland attempts to shield us from this, but in fact it makes it clear.

One key criticism of Baudrillard is relevant here. In 1991 his article 'The Reality Gulf' was published in *The Guardian*. In this article, as

Christopher Norris represents it, Baudrillard took as his focus the Gulf War, and argued that

> we had lost all sense of the difference – or the point of transition – between a war of words, a mass-media simulation conducted (supposedly) by way of preparing us for 'the real thing', and the thing itself which would likewise 'take place' only in the minds and imaginations of a captive TV audience, bombarded with the same sorts of video-games imagery that had filled their screens during the build-up campaign.

For Norris this absence of the 'real' in Baudrillard's thought is not only 'sheer nonsense', with Baudrillard representing, he argues, 'the most visible [symptom] of a widespread cultural malaise', it is also highly suspect. By declaring that 'we now inhabit a realm of purely fictive or illusory appearances' we can ignore, or cease to feel, anything like empathy for the very real suffering that took place during the Gulf War, much of which – the suffering of Iraqi civilians, for example – was not necessarily given the same amount of coverage in the Western media as the Allies' bombing of military installations.[64]

So how does fake fur fit into this kind of debate? Like Baudrillard's simulations, fake fur represents fur, it makes up for the absence of fur by reproducing it, faking it. We know this. But we can go further. In fake fur what is acknowledged is that the real – the animal – is gone, and what we are left with is a simulation of a simulation. Most of us never experience, or truly engage with, the reality of the death of the animal. What we engage with is a coat. Real fur, following this logic, is always already hyperreal, and any debates about the ethics of wearing fur are a resort to a claim to access reality that is always fraudulent. In this sense, fake fur would appear to be a truly postmodern response to the debates about fur. To concentrate on the 'real', on the welfare of the animal, is to retreat into some kind of hinterland of philosophy that is always already false.

While this argument fits into certain streams of postmodern philosophy, I am not happy with it. Beyond this, in the realm of the real (in which I firmly believe), there lurks a problem with fake fur. This is spelt out by Julia Szabo: 'One reason people may be feeling more at ease wearing fur is that it is becoming harder for fur lovers and haters to tell the difference between real and fake.'[65] This might appear to support the postmodern hypothesis that there is no distinction between simulation and reality, because reality is always already a simulation, but such an interpretation hides the ethical impact of this loss of difference. Spray-painting a fur coat in protest can become difficult if it is impossible to tell the difference between real and fake, and this makes it, perhaps, more likely that wearing fur is safer, less likely to elicit comments and protests. Going further than this, the fashion industry's increasing use of dyed fur also boosts the possibility of using animal skins in fashion. As the designer Anna Molinari notes, 'Coloured fur could be mistaken for fake fur.'[66] What may appear to be a parody, a simulation of a simulation if you like, returns to us as something more than that. Fake fur may actually support the wearing of fur rather than offer an alternative to it.

Just as Ham's smile may not be a smile, and as a pet may not be an animal, so fur may be fake fur, and vice versa. On the surface of our relationship with animals exist a number of conundrums that we often choose to ignore, when, in fact, we may learn more about animals – and about ourselves – if we consider them more fully. An animal may look like – what? Something different, something the same, something not like an animal at all. If we trace the source of this confusion back to the being doing the looking – us – we may be in a position to challenge some of the customary ways in which we live with animals.

This is an issue that hasn't been touched on yet. So far, I have been assuming a fixed and stable status for the human in the face of an ambiguous and fluid one for the animal. Animals can become meat, coats, blank pages on which we, secure in our species, record our desires. However, we live in a world where the epithet 'animal' is constantly being applied to those who might otherwise appear to have human status. Murderers, war criminals: these animals, we are told, are less than human. They lack, it would seem, some of the qualities that make us what we are. The category of the animal is used as a shorthand for the failure of humanity: over-indulgence in food can turn one into a 'pig'. Loss of reason, whether evinced through alcohol consumption, power or psychosis, brings out the beast that, it would seem, is always lurking beneath the surface. But this slippage into the realm of the animal is always figured as metaphorical. We don't really become an animal, but some of the perceived qualities of the animal are given to us. This metaphorical interpretation of the slide from human to animal has not always been the case, and an older argument about wearing fur can offer a glimpse of another danger, not, this time, to our conceptualization of the boundary between animal and human, but to the status of the human being itself.

Dressing up as a Human

In 1633 the puritanical critic of the theatre, William Prynne, launched an attack on cross-dressing. In a period in which women were not allowed onto the public stage, the women's parts were always played by boys, and this, Prynne argued, could cause moral danger to the spectator.[67] Cross-dressing, however, was not the end of his complaint. There was something worse, something even more dangerous than a boy dressing up as a woman. Prynne wrote, 'And must it not then be man's sin and shame to act a beast, or bear his image, with which he hath no proportion? What is this but to obliterate that most glorious image which God himself hath stamped on us, to strip us of our excellency, and to prove worse than brutes?' It is by dressing as animals that 'the shape of reasonable men [is changed] into the likeness of unreasonable beasts and creatures'.[68] In dressing as animals we destroy our own status. What is revealed in Prynne's attack on the stage is a sense that human status, which we might assume to be absolute and unquestionable, was figured as dangerously fragile. If dress can upset species stability, it doesn't say a great deal about the strength of that stability.

Prynne was writing over 300 years ago, but his representation of human frailty remains present in different forms today. As the next two chapters will attempt to show, some of the ways in which we assert our difference from animals are breaking down. A new sense of animal intelligence, and of animals' physical similarity to humans, for example, go towards making the relation more and more complex, and if in addition to that we also recognize ourselves as unstable entities then the relation becomes even more complicated. We now have evolutionary theory rather than Prynne's somewhat mystical account of human decline to remind us of the inseparability of humans and animals, but we also have very different conceptions of the moral place of animals.

In the thirteenth century the theologian Thomas Aquinas argued that cruelty to animals was not wrong in itself, but that animals should be 'loved from charity as good things we wish others to have, in that by charity we cherish this for God's honour and man's service'.[69] For Aquinas, a person who was cruel to animals was more likely to be cruel to humans, and treating animals with kindness was a preparation to treat humans well, and was a way of securing your own place in heaven; the animal itself was not important. Prynne seems to follow this logic. The sin in dressing up as an animal – which, in all likelihood, involved fur – was a sin because of its affect upon human status, not upon the animal. Since that time moral arguments about the welfare of animals have shifted their focus. It is the animal's right not to be abused that is central to our discussions, whether we see it as such or not: the RSPCA does not prosecute offenders in order to help them lead blameless lives, it prosecutes in defence of the animals who are abused. But, despite this key shift, some of Prynne's argument remains relevant. During the sixteenth and seventeenth centuries the human was central to God's creation (a status given by the Bible); alongside this, new philosophical arguments emerged to offer further evidence for human power. Human status was reiterated in humanist thought and in the New Scientific philosophy of Francis Bacon and René Descartes (I return to their work in the next chapter). Reason was once again established as the realm of the human: in fact, for Descartes, it was what made us distinct. In the late eighteenth century the American Declaration of Independence formulated the human in a slightly different way by arguing that 'man' had certain inalienable rights, such as 'life, liberty and the pursuit of happiness' (and in the mid-nineteenth century Harriet Taylor Mill was to question the limitation of these rights to men). To say that a right is inalienable is to say that without those rights human status cannot be; is to say that, if those rights are gone, so too is the human. The human here becomes a being with an essential status that is fixed, stable. Only when infringing the rights of another human (by, for example, assaulting them) do we forfeit our own inalienable rights, and lose our liberty. An animal, you may recall, cannot be a criminal, as a criminal must have intent. By extension, an animal does not have inalienable rights, for if they did all meat-eaters might find themselves behind bars.

This kind of thinking about the human is often labelled 'humanist'. The philosopher Kate Soper sees humanist ideas as appealing '(positively) to the notion of a core humanity or common essential feature in terms of which human beings can be defined and understood'.[70] More recent philosophical discussions have begun to unravel this idea of the human, and what emerged in the late twentieth century is what has been termed 'posthumanism', a philosophical crisis in the conceptualization of humanity. In 1997 Jacques Derrida outlined one of the problems facing posthumanist humanity. What, Derrida asks, is 'proper to man'? That is, what is it that defines the human as human (as opposed to animal, machine and so on)?

He cites the conventional responses – 'speech, reason, the logos, history, laughing, mourning, burial, the gift, etc.' – but regards the proliferation of proofs, the fact that there is no one thing that makes us human, as evidence that it is not in the possession of one thing – the ability to speak, for example – but in the 'configuration' of all of those traits that the property of the human can be found. 'For that reason,' he writes, what is proper to man 'can never be limited to a single trait and it is never closed; structurally speaking it can attract a non-finite number of other concepts, beginning with the concept of a concept.'[71] Such a recognition of the limitless properties of humanity is not regarded by Derrida as a positive outcome, rather, it shows that proving ourselves to be different from animals can take on comic proportions: it is everything and nothing simultaneously.

Later in the same essay Derrida does, however, offer one place where the human is distinguished from the animal. But his definition carries with it, almost inevitably, an inherently destructive force. Bestiality is one of the worst crimes that a human can commit – in the seventeenth century it was regarded as 'a sin against God, nature and the law' (three strikes in one, you might say).[72] It is the place where the isolation of humanity is destroyed. And yet, for Derrida, it is also truly the property of man: 'beasts', he writes, 'are in any case exempt by definition' from bestiality. 'One cannot speak . . . of the *bêtise* or bestiality of an animal.'[73] An animal will always engage in sexual intercourse with another animal; only a human, therefore, can be a bestialist. This is not quite the same as claiming that only a human has the capacity to think. Prynne's fears for humans dressed as animals offer, then, a historical and visual version of a contemporary philosophical problem. What is it that makes us human? Or, perhaps that question should be rephrased: what is it that makes us not animal?

An image contemporary with Prynne's argument takes this even further (and it may be that this kind of costuming was the real source of Prynne's complaint). When, in the early seventeenth century, Inigo Jones sketched a

design for a costume for 'a bird' (see above) for a performance at the court of Charles I, he was creating a spectacle. But if we place his illustration within the frame of Prynne's argument we can perhaps begin to see something more threatening. It is an inversion of what we encountered at the beginning of this chapter. Ham smiles, and we see ourselves: we put on a disguise, and we lose ourselves. The sketchy quality of this image – Jones also created more detailed costumes for a lion, ape, fox, ass and hog – echoes the emerging sketchiness of the human. A few strokes of the pen and a transformation has taken place. From bird-man to ape-astronaut, from transformed humanity to fake fur, we have travelled over 300 years, but we can see that we are little further forward. In fact, in Jones's image the idea that we never look into a chicken's eyes and see ourselves seems to be undermined: a look in the mirror might reveal a contiguity that is terrifying. But, as with the image of Ham, we rarely look properly.

CHAPTER TWO

Real and Symbolic: Questions of Difference

In 1895 Francis Barraud, a photographer by trade, painted a picture of his brother Mark's dog Nipper (see opposite). Nipper was part bull terrier, part fox terrier; by no means a pedigree dog like those immortalized by artists in the growing number of nineteenth-century breeding manuals.[1] Those books celebrated the purity of dog breeds. Barraud's image, on the other hand, presented something rather different. Here, the dog was listening; it was engaging with the machinery of the human world in just the way a human would. This dog is more than an exhibit on the popular dog-show circuit, he is represented as fully partaking of his human surroundings.

Barraud's image has become one of the most famous animal paintings in the world, thanks to its use as the trademark of RCA Victor and the HMV shop chain. But the transformation of private image to public trademark involved some important changes. When Barraud finished the painting, he was unsatisfied. The horn he had used was too dark, and he approached the Gramophone Co. Ltd in London to borrow a brass horn. Here Barraud was asked by the owner of the company, William Barry Owen, to replace the original cylinder phonograph with a gramophone.

Barraud obliged, and the original machine was painted over with its more modern counterpart. The image was then used by the Gramophone Co. as its trademark. Despite updating the technology in the image, however, Nipper remained as he always had been, listening.

The image conjures up an ideal of the animal that opens up the debates that are the focus of this chapter. Somewhere in this famous picture we can trace two apparently antithetical ideas: similarity and absolute difference. The first of these – similarity – is the most obvious: this is a dog with the capacity to listen, not just to hear: it is an active rather than passive participant in its world. We know that dogs listen – to cars, other dogs, approaching humans and so on. But this dog is listening to something that is not present in reality. It is listening to a virtual noise. The leap from reality to virtual reality, from an approaching human to a televisual representation of an approaching human, is one that we often believe that only humans can make. Indeed, in an essay on primate communication, Clarence Ray Carpenter, one of the fathers of primatology, seems to make exactly this discovery. Carpenter writes of the recording and replaying of gibbon communication to the gibbons and notes: 'Generally, the reactions of gibbons to reproductions of their own voices were very like the reactions that they would have made to another intruding group of gibbons; there was exploratory and aggressive behavior. I got the impression, too, that the group was confused by their own recorded sounds that were returned to them.'[2] This is presented, I think, as a failing on the part of the animals. The gibbons cannot tell the difference between a tape of themselves (virtual reality) and the approach of another group of gibbons (reality). Nipper's stance next to the horn of the gramophone might appear to question this distinction. This dog is listening as we might listen: with pleasure, with attentiveness. Where the gibbons look for a physical presence to correspond to the voices, Nipper merely listens.

The familiar title of the picture – *His Master's Voice* – however, offers a very different notion of the dog's response. Where the picture represents the possibility of a dog engaging in what would be understood as a human activity – listening for pleasure – he is simultaneously enacting his inferiority by listening for dominion, for his *master*'s voice. The possibility of an animal engaging with music is pictured in such a way that human superiority is reinscribed: even as the dog appears to be more than a dog, to be able to recognize the possibility of pleasure without body, it is reinforcing the status quo. More than this, the fact that this dog is listening to a formless noise, listening for his master's voice, would imply that dominion, the relation that gives humans absolute mastery over animals, is innate to the animal itself. This dog does not need the physical presence of its master to listen to his voice: the voice is effective without a body. Being mastered is a natural and internalized part of the animal's life. And, as the alterations made to Barraud's image seem to show, we could also argue that being mastered transcends other cultural and technological changes.

The image of Nipper listening is one that most of us would recognize immediately. But what we might forget as we look at a carrier bag or a shop front is how we might read this image against itself. The dog is listening, just as we are about to listen to our CDs, but the dog is also enacting the 'natural' order: the master's voice is all. The rest of this chapter looks at other paradoxes of similarity and difference. The use of animals in children's literature is an old one, and is one that opens up ideas about how we wish to live with animals. These books voice a desire, a desire that, in adulthood, becomes melancholy. The relation of humans to animals often presented in books has been developed in film, and in a brief look at the changing face of the non-human in this medium, some of the difficulties and dangers of giving animals what are perceived to be 'human' traits can be illustrated. I then turn to the use of animals in science, and to what might be regarded as an absolutely different mode of understanding. I want to draw some uncomfortable parallels between literature, film and science, and to suggest the possibility that the ways in which we think about animals in these three areas are not wholly distinct. I begin with childhood.

Children and Animals

In *Totem and Taboo* Sigmund Freud looked at the ways in which what he termed 'primitive' peoples understood the world around them. He wrote:

> There is a great deal of resemblance between the relations of children and of primitive men towards animals. Children show no trace of the arrogance which urges adult civilized men to draw a hard-and-fast line between their own nature and that of all other animals. Children have no scruples over allowing the avowal of their bodily needs, they no doubt feel themselves more akin to animals than their elders, who may well be a puzzle to them.[3]

For Freud this closeness between the child and animals was frequently breached by neurosis, by the appearance of fear in the child for one particular, often previously loved, species. But on a more immediate level, Freud's recognition that childhood is a time in which animals are of particular, and specific, value, is an important one, and is one that can be traced in the constant presence of animals in books written for children. As Karin Lesnik-Oberstein has estimated, 'at least two-thirds of the books [available in children's bookshops] are in some form or another linked with nature and the environment, and – specifically and most importantly – with animals'.[4] The question of the child's lack of arrogance that Freud finds is certainly central to many of the classic children's books of the last century, and I will look at a few of them, and examine how they work, and what the representation of animals within them might mean. The different forms of anthropomorphism present in these books offer different possibilities for our relationship with animals.

The Wind in the Willows is, according to the jacket of my childhood edition, 'the best-loved children's book of the twentieth century'.[5] Written by Kenneth Grahame, then Secretary of the Bank of England, the book was based on stories told, and letters written, to Grahame's son, Alastair. First published in 1908, it tells the story of the riverbank community, but it is never clear whether the animals, Ratty, Mole, Toad, Badger, and the evil weasels, are, as Neil Philip notes, 'humanized animals – or animalized humans'.[6] The story, with its mixture of animals of animal size and of human, offers no attempt at reality. One of E. H. Shepherd's illustrations shows actual-sized Mole and Ratty pulling on the harness of a, by comparison, massive full-sized horse while, a few pages later, Mr Toad is able to steal and drive away a human car. The book mixes the reality of its representation of the countryside with the fiction of a world of speaking animals. In literary terms, *The Wind in the Willows* fits into the genre of 'magic realism', 'a kind of modern fiction in which fabulous and fantastical events are included in a narrative that otherwise maintains the "reliable" tone of objective realistic report'.[7] Ultimately, however, the world of the riverbank is an idealized picture of human society. Toad's abandonment of the caravan for the motorcar – 'Glorious, stirring sight! . . . The *only* way to travel!' – is represented as a disintegration of 'true' living. The car represents the overturning of rural ways of life, and the threatening arrival of modernity, and takes with it on its journey not only the true, natural order of time – 'Here to-day – in next week to-morrow!'[8] – but also the true, natural order of community. It destroys the rural idyll: Toad Hall falls into the hands of weasels and stoats, and the Lord of the Manor is reduced to the status of a car thief, who is forced to dress as a laundry woman to escape from prison.

The disorder of the impact of modernity is, however, limited. By the end of the book the 'natural' order is reinstated, with the rebels kicked out of Toad Hall and its rightful owner reinstated. But what is clear is that we have not experienced a natural world at all, but a parable about the dangers of modernity, translated into the voices of animals. In this *The Wind in the Willows* is not unlike a collection like *Aesop's Fables*, in that the tale told is ultimately about 'us' and not 'them'. As well as this, Grahame's message, embedded in the adventures of Mole, Ratty and the others, is ultimately a deeply reactionary one. Toad, who clearly shows no merit as Lord of the Manor, is returned to his Hall anyway, because it is his rightful inheritance. He may be very poor at performing his social role, but his return is a viewed as a return of stability, of the old ways of history. The animals are the vehicles for a conservative philosophy, just as, in *Aesop's Fables*, they were vehicles for moral teaching.

The anthropomorphism on display in *The Wind in the Willows* is an all-encompassing one. When humans do appear – the gaoler, the train driver, the bargewoman – they engage with the animals as if they were human. At Toad's trial the Chairman of the Bench of Magistrates refers to him as an 'incorrigible rogue and hardened ruffian'.[9] The fact that he is also a toad appears to escape the magistrate's notice. Here we are immersed in Grahame's creation. We cannot enjoy the tale and simultaneously doubt the world in which it takes place: to do so would be to destroy the narrative altogether. Instead we are asked to, and most of us do, readily accept the world of the riverbank as a world we recognize. Animals are like us, in fact, the line between the bargewoman and the toad does not exist: the animals are us. This is anthropomorphism at its most extreme, and, paradoxically, at its most invisible. We forget that the animals are animals.

This is not, however, the only way in which animals are represented in children's books. Another classic, E. B. White's *Charlotte's Web* (1952), offers a very different picture of the animal world, and it is a picture that, in many ways, supports Freud's ideas about the relation between children and animals. In this book the farmyard, like Grahame's riverbank, is a pseudo-human society. The pig converses with a spider, a rat and geese. But rather than this being the only world that there is, we have, in *Charlotte's Web*, the sense of separation of human from animal: there is another world, another conversation going on among people. The intermediary between these two worlds is, of course, a child: Fern. *Charlotte's Web* tells the story of how a spider, Charlotte, contrives to save a piglet, Wilbur, from slaughter, the usual fate of his species. Charlotte creates apparent miracles by writing various messages in her web: 'Some Pig', 'Terrific', 'Humble'. Because of these messages Wilbur becomes a celebrity, with crowds coming from miles around to see him. He becomes more valuable alive than dead, and so is saved from the knife.

In *Charlotte's Web* White simultaneously asks his readers to believe that animals can speak to each other, but also makes it clear that we, his readers, are privileged to hear them. Only Fern among all the humans in the book is able to understand what is going on in the animal world. None of the adults – Mr and Mrs Arable, Fern's parents, Mr and Mrs Zuckerman, Fern's aunt and uncle – and none of the other children can hear the conversation in the barn. As readers we share in Fern's access to the world of the farmyard. This leads to some interesting, and self-conscious, debates in the book. Mrs Arable says to her husband, 'I worry about Fern . . . Did you hear that way she rambled on about the animals, pretending that they talked?' Mr Arable's reply offers two interpretations of his daughter's belief that the animals talk (and, of course, we *know* that they do: we, the readers, 'hear' them too). First of all he blames it on his daughter's 'lively imagination' (something regarded as a typical and healthy part of childhood), but he also notes, 'Maybe our ears aren't as sharp as Fern's.'[10] There is a sense of melancholy here, a sense of a recognition that adulthood brings with it a loss, a distance from the natural world that can never be bridged. Part of growing up, it seems, entails a growing away from animals. The fact that Wilbur was to be slaughtered, first by Mr Avery as the runt of the litter, and then by Mr Zuckerman for food, attests to the impact of this division between human and animal worlds. The communication across the species is only possible in a world where an equilibrium is perceived. Where dominion is in place such conversations cease to be possible. Only children lack, in Freud's terms, the 'arrogance' that upsets the natural peace.

So, there are two forms of anthropomorphism in place already here: one all-encompassing, where humans and animals are equal, and the other where there is an equality that only the child (and the reader) can understand. The latter is a much more troubling version, as it offers us the possibility that we may lose, or may already have lost something, and because of this loss we may be living lives that are more directly destructive than we can imagine. If we could hear animals speak to each other, could we still do what we do to them?

In another children's classic, Eric Knight's *Lassie Come-Home*, we get a different version of anthropomorphism once again. In this book, as in the film, we are told the story of the bond between a collie and Joe Carraclough, the son of her original owner. When the dog is sold to help the Carraclough family weather the storm of the father's unemployment, Lassie keeps escaping from her new home and returning to the school gates to meet Joe. Each time the dog is returned to her new owner, The Duke of Rudling, but again and again, she contrives to escape and return 'home'. Eventually the Duke takes Lassie to his estate in the north of Scotland, but once again the dog escapes, and makes her way slowly back to North Yorkshire to Joe. The journey home is interspersed with events: Lassie is almost shot as a sheep-worrier, she is captured by dog-catchers, she spends some time with a travelling pedlar, but ultimately, it is the idea of home that drives her on.

Knight does not anthropomorphize the dog in the way that White anthropomorphizes the pig and the spider in *Charlotte's Web*. In a pseudo-documentary style, he tells a tale of a natural world new to both reader and dog. In this world the dog learns to fear men, to avoid them, and to survive without their help, and we learn to understand and share in the experience of this dog. When another animal is encountered our understanding comes through Knight's translation of their animal noises, rather than through their humanized conversation. On the first night of her journey Lassie encounters another dog: 'Perhaps he was friendly,' Knight notes.

But he was not. He came tearing up the path, his mane erect, his ears flat. Lassie crouched to meet him. As he sprang, she stepped aside. He turned, giving loud voice in hysterical rage. His tones were saying: 'This is my home – you are an intruder. It is my home and I will defend it.'[11]

We get no conversation, as we get in the other books, we merely get a human interpretation of a canine situation. The dog's bark is roughly translated into human language by the narrator. This narrator sees inside the minds of the humans – Joe, Mr Carraclough, the Duke – but he also sees into the minds of the animals. In this sense the dog is given a thought process (although Knight makes it clear how different from the human thought process this is), but is also, like Nipper, given an innate love of mastery. Lassie wants to come home, wants to return to her true master; wants to be mastered.

But, again, as in *Charlotte's Web*, *Lassie Come-Home* offers us a melancholy sense of the loss of communication between adult and animal. Having travelled some way with Rowlie, a pedlar, Lassie goes her own way: Rowlie heads east, Lassie goes south. At their parting Rowlie notes the dog's intelligence – 'ye understand a lot, don't ye?' – and rues his own lack: 'Nay, that's the pity of it. Ye can understand some o' man's language, but man isn't bright enough to understand thine. And yet it's us that's supposed to be most intelligent!'[12] What this book gives us is a chance for some understanding, a chance to transcend some of the barriers that exist between human and animal. Just as the book and film offer what Marjorie Garber terms 'the "Lassie principle"' – 'the power of the lost-and-found, the lost-in-order-to-be-found, the found-only-to-be-lost-again'[13] – the story of *Lassie Come-Home* also reminds us of the powerful desire of all humans – children and adults – to get into the minds of animals. The all-pervasive presence of animals in children's literature would seem to emphasize this point. What Knight's novel gives us, however, is a form of anthropomorphism that is limited in its scope. We do not fully comprehend Lassie, but we get some kind of insight. The narrator of the story notes: 'She was a dog, and she would not think in terms of thoughts such as we may put in words. There was only a growing desire that was at first vague . . .'[14] The conversation that Lassie has with herself is lost to us forever in this book, it is untranslatable into our language: and yet we get something of her interior life. More realist than magic realism, *Lassie Come-Home* recognizes the difficulty of the world of animals, but still argues that communicating some of it is possible.

But, there is a question that all three texts (and many, many others) ask. Why is it that these other beings are so central to the child's engagement with the world? Animals in books speak to us, sometimes literally. The reason for this centrality of representations of animals in these books might be that they offer a fulfilment of one of the key desires of our lives. This is a desire that begins with ease in childhood and which becomes – as the adults in some of these book show – more and more complex and melancholy with age. We might argue that the desire to comprehend and communicate with animals is infantile, but if we do not have these narratives of communication (and not all of those narratives are written down, of course) then we will lose contact with a large part of our world. If I cannot say that a dog is sad, what can I say that it is? In a sense, without anthropomorphism we are unable to comprehend and represent the presence of an animal. This is one of the problems of anthropomorphism that needs to be explored. We may regard the humanization of animals that takes place in many narratives as sentimental, but without it the only relation we can have with animals is a very distant, and perhaps mechanistic one. As well as this, anthropomorphism might actually serve an ethical function: if we don't believe that in some way we can communicate with and understand animals, what is to make us stop and think as we experiment upon them, eat them, put them in cages? By gaining access to the world of animals, these books offer a way of thinking about human–animal relations more generally, and potentially more positively.

The different forms of anthropomorphism in these books, though, present problems for the status of humans. If, through whichever mode of anthropomorphism, an animal can be represented as being like us, then an important line between the species has been eroded. But this can be a double-edged sword. Just as a pet nearly always 'says' what we want it to say, so the fictionalized animals present a world in which we, humans, remain central: while Lassie may have a mind of her own, it is a mind that drives her back to her true 'master'. We can, though, read this in reverse: where the stories may represent an extension of a world that we can control, in our desire that animals should be for us, that we should have dominion, one that includes understanding, we might actually be undoing that dominion. In our desire to rectify the loss of communication with the non-human world we may in fact be upsetting the human one. This danger is something that has persisted across history. We can turn to the seventeenth century to see a version of this that sets out the difficulty very clearly.

In 1616 Ben Jonson wrote a conventional 'country house poem', 'To Penshurst'. A country house poem was traditionally written in celebration of the power and status of a poet's patrons, in this case, Sir Robert Sidney, Viscount Lisle. In 'To Penshurst' Jonson, following the convention, presents a world of perfect order, where humans are very clearly on top, with Sidney himself at the top of the human chain. This is a representation of an ideal world that does honour to its master. Here animals serve a clear function: they are for use by man. The pheasant, Jonson writes, is 'willing to be kill'd'.[15] This is a representation of absolute dominion, of an animal offering itself for slaughter. It comes, however, at a price. If a pheasant is willing to be killed, doesn't that mean that it has a will? Such a suggestion undermines the assumption of the absolute difference between human and animal that the dominion appears to exhibit. Even as it serves (or is served on a plate) the animal upsets dominion. Anthropocentrism leads to anthropomorphism, which in turn upsets the possibility of *anthropos* as a separate and distinct category.

A similar danger can be traced in the varied use of animals in writing for children. If animals are indistinguishable from humans, or equal to humans, where is the difference? This is a question raised by the representation of animals in children's books, but it is perhaps in film, in the visual representation of the animal, that greater dangers exist. Here, while we are still dealing in fiction, we are dealing in a fiction that looks real. Where Nipper may have crossed the border that says that only humans can imagine and engage with virtual worlds in his concentration on the bodiless sounds coming from the gramophone, humans cross a different border in a similar medium. Only we can engage with the worlds represented on the cinema screen as if they were real, but when those worlds depict animals it is often difficult to see how a boundary between human and animal can be maintained.

Filming Animals

In his book *The Story of Lassie* the wonderfully named Rudd B. Weatherwax, original trainer of Pal, the dog who played Lassie in a sequence of films in the 1940s and '50s, offers two intertwined histories: one of the history of the dog generally, and one of the history of dogs in films. I'll begin with the latter, as Weatherwax does, and then move on to the former, as, for Weatherwax, the appearance of the dog in the cinema is a crucial development in canine evolution.

There are, he argues, four eras of dogs in cinema. In the first, the early 1920s, dogs like Brownie, 'the original "wonder dog" of the movies', Jiggs, a Boston bulldog, and Pal, a black and white terrier were used for comic effect: 'dogs smoked cigars, they read books, they always were getting into mischief'. These comic dogs were replaced in the next era by German Shepherds: first was Strongheart, and then, in the mid to late 1920s, came the reign of Rin-Tin-Tin.[16] A synopsis of one of Rinty's silent films, *The Night Cry* (1926), from the dog's website gives a sense of the nature of his work. This dog is certainly not smoking a cigar. 'A giant condor is killing sheep and Rinty is unjustly accused and by the law of the range must be destroyed. Rinty's owner hides him from the other ranchers. The condor steals a child and Rinty tracks it to its lair and destroys the giant bird.' The synopsis goes on: 'All the stories of how Rin-Tin-Tin could really act are substantiated in this film.'[17] As well as starring in 23 silent films, Rinty also crossed over into the talkies seven times. In his films we have moved from the comic potential of the dog as sub-human to the dramatic possibility of dog as truly 'man's best friend'.

For Weatherwax, the next stage of development in cinema, the 1930s and '40s, is the era of smaller dogs, such as Daisy and Asta, the pets in, respectively, the *Blondie* and *Thin Man* series. Asta, played by Skippy, a wire terrier, was trained by Weatherwax. In this era, however, he argues, 'film bypassed the genuine dog stories'. By implication, a film with a dog that merely helped its owners to sniff out clues (Asta), or followed its owners from room to room (Daisy), was not a genuine dog story, whereas, for Weatherwax, the *Lassie* films were. And it is these latter that represent Weatherwax's fourth era in dog-cinema. Lassie, he notes, had a huge impact. By 1947, within four years of Lassie's debut, 'there were approximately 250 trained dogs working in motion pictures . . . During this period it was estimated that Hollywood studios paid $250,000 annually for their canine actors!'[18] We are still living in a post-Lassie world.

But the history of dogs in cinema does not only represent a development in film itself, with the emergence of talkies seeing a decline for dog actors (writers, Weatherwax notes, 'couldn't write smart dialog for a non-human, so they left them out of the main action').[19] The history of dogs in cinema also plays an important part in the history of dogs *per se*. Where there were four eras of dogs in cinema, there are, Weatherwax argues, six stages in the dog's development more generally. Moving through the historical development of the dog as hunter, tender of flocks, guard of the master's home, and as pet, he sees entertainment as the apex of evolution.

> Finally, and only after progressing through each of the five preceding stages of his development, [the dog] took an important place in show business, first in tent shows and the circus, then in vaudeville, and most recently in motion pictures. Each era can be divided further into different stages, such as the various canine phases in entertainment leading up to the appearance on the scene of Lassie.[20]

Lassie becomes, for his trainer, the high-point in the development of the dog. It is as if all of history had led up to Pal's transformation in 1943.

In reality, though, despite Weatherwax's great claims for Lassie, the history of animals in film pre-dates his interpretation. As Jonathan Burt has shown, animals played an integral part in the development of moving film as a medium. From the sequential photographs of horses taken by Eadweard Muybridge in the 1870s, animals were, Burt argues, 'an important motive force in driving the new technology of moving film as well as being, in some senses, its inspiration'. One of the first moving films ever made was shot at London Zoo by the Lumière brothers, and shown in February 1896.[21]

So what did Lassie have that other animal stars lacked? Why might his/her (Pal was male, Lassie female) trainer regard 1943 as such a high-point in the history of the dog? According to Weatherwax, a genuine dog story was one reason (but of course, this 'genuine' story was based on a novel). As well as this, Lassie – as Pal was swiftly renamed – also had 'personality'. It is somewhat strange to think that Lassie was also the star of the imaginatively titled *Lassie Show*, which was broadcast on the radio between 1947 and 1950. S/he supplied 'all the barks, whines, and growls demanded by the script'.[22] And, something Weatherwax doesn't mention, 'two animal imitators filled in when Lassie missed a cue or doubled as other dogs in the script'.[23] What Weatherwax's biography of Lassie does show, however, is that this dog had a real talent. The last third of his book is given over to training techniques: how to turn your dog into a film star. Taking the reader through elementary school, high school, and on to college, Weatherwax, with the aid of photographs, outlines his methods of training Lassie to perform certain tricks. These range from coming when called and walking to heel (elementary), sitting up, rolling over, playing dead, and – my favourite – saying a prayer (high school), through to the more complex crawling, acting like a lame dog, acting exhausted, climbing a ladder and sneezing. The silent cues used on the film set are included in the book for the future movie star to follow.

We might be cynical about the idea of training a dog to say a prayer (who, apart from the Spanish Inquisition, would have thought spirituality could be taught with the aid of a leash?). What is clear from Weatherwax's book, though, is that Lassie, and other screen dogs who have followed him/her, are highly intelligent creatures. It's worth quoting a section from Weatherwax's book to underline this. Is your pet another Lassie? he asks. Here's how to find out:

> Let's give him a little test – this scene from Lassie's first motion picture, 'Lassie Come Home.'
>
> Use your living room as the 'set.' Place two of your friends in chairs on opposite sides of it. Select a spot in one corner, commanding a view of the entire room, as the location for your imaginary camera, and remember that you must stay behind it. And you mustn't say a word – this is a modern, sound motion picture.
>
> Now, here is the scene; remember it? Lassie has been rescued from near death after swimming the river, and had been nursed back to health by the elderly couple that had taken him into their

house. With his strength returning, he once more was feeling the urge to return home to his young master. Four o'clock, the hour when he always met the boy, strikes, and the urge becomes stronger. And now, your camera is turning. Your dog, emulating Lassie, is lying on his side on the floor in the center of the room. 'Quiet! Action! Camera!'

Your dog looks up, suddenly alert. He gets to his feet, whines, and goes first to one of your friends, and then to the other. Restlessly, he goes to the door, scratches at it. Then he tries to open it by the knob, but it is locked. He stands looking at the door, then back to your friends, and barks. They don't move, so he walks briskly, impatiently back to them, first nudging the elbow of one with his nose, then putting a paw up pleadingly on the knee of the other. They still don't show a sign of understanding his language, so he goes to the window, puts his front paws up on the window seat, and, looking out, gives a bark. Once more he returns to your friends, but his pause in front of them is even more brief this time, as he fairly runs back to the door. He barks again, and looks back to your friends with a despairing glance that can leave his wish in doubt no longer.

'Cut!' And that's the end of the scene, and of your dog's test. How did he do? Probably not too well, but don't feel discouraged. Lassie managed it, even though at that point in his career he had learned not more than half the lessons that follow [in the book].[24]

I may be cynical about the possibility of teaching a dog to pray, but Pal/Lassie's skill as a performer is hard to deny.

We begin to confront the problem that was faced with anthropomorphic children's literature. While the stories told in *The Wind in the Willows*, *Charlotte's Web* and *Lassie Come-Home* may emphasize in different ways the equivalence of human and animal, so the skill of the trained animal on display in film is a reminder, not of their servitude and inferiority, but of their capacity. Where in fables animals teach humans morals, in film this process is reversed and animals reveal their capacity to learn. We are returned to Peter Singer's somewhat uncomfortable suggestion that, if notions of use-value are based upon capacities such as communication through language, then human infants could as well be used for experimental purposes as animals (linguistic limitations may be another possible link between children and animals). Children, of course, have the capacity to develop, to learn; animals, we would seem to be arguing as we regard them as inferior to ourselves, do not. They are limited to their innate, instinctual abilities. Lassie would appear to give the lie to this suggestion.

So, somewhere between the childhood relationship with animals, the fictional representation of them, and the cinematic skills they display, our relationship with animals is simultanoeously upset and reinforced. The links made in childhood are gone, and animal inferiority is reiterated. We learn to separate ourselves from our beastly servants; we come to understand, and live by our superiority. This is something that, I think, lies at the heart of the classic Disney film, *Old Yeller* (1957). This film, one of Disney's first forays into live-action, tells the story of Travis Coates's coming of age. At the beginning of the story, set in post-Civil War Texas, Jim Coates, the head of the household, heads off on a three-month cattle drive. He leaves his wife and two sons, and hands the running of the farm over to the oldest, fifteen-year-old Travis, who is also told to keep an eye on his younger brother, Arliss. Almost as soon as the father has gone, a stray dog, Old Yeller, turns up and wreaks havoc. But Arliss has taken to the dog, and, despite Travis's concerns (well-founded it would seem when the dog steals a side of venison) the dog becomes an integral part of the new family set-up. He defends all of its members: Arliss from an angry she-bear, Travis from some wild hogs, and mother from a rabid wolf. Tragically, however, Old Yeller is bitten by the wolf and, after a long wait, it becomes clear that the dog too has rabies and must be destroyed. Travis shoots his own beloved dog. For this reason Jerry C. Kutner calls *Old Yeller* 'surely one of the most disturbing "children's movies" in cinema history'.[25]

Old Yeller is a very interesting representation of the limitations of the child's relations with animals. Here the younger son, Arliss, is quickly dispossessed of the pet dog, as the older son, Travis, gains a work-mate, and at the end of the film, Travis's shooting of the beloved dog is a kind of liminal moment between childhood and adulthood. Travis has passed the test he was set by his father, he has run the farm and protected the family, and his helper is no longer needed. The father returns the day after Old Yeller has been shot with a new horse for Travis, and it is, as promised at the beginning of the film, an adult's rather than a child's horse. To emphasize Travis's journey into adulthood, at the very end of the film we see that his apparent emotional attachment to Old Yeller is dismissed as Old Yeller's pup, Young Yeller, comes to replace the lost companion. This disturbing film (imagine having to shoot your own dog), while using the familiar trope of the relationship between the child and the animal also recognizes that that relationship cannot and should not last. At the end of *Old Yeller* the newly mature Travis has learned that all dogs are interchangeable, that an animal may die, but that animals live on. This, it would seem, is how we as adults should think.

Some dialogue from the film underscores the division between child and adult. This scene follows Travis's shooting of Rose, the rabid family cow:

Arliss: Where'll Rose go now she's dead?
Travis: Nowhere, I reckon. She's just dead.
Arliss: Will she go to heaven?
Travis: I don't much reckon.
Arliss: Ain't there no cows in heaven for the angels to milk?
Travis: Well, how do I know? . . .

Where Arliss asks about cows in heaven, Travis has learned that an animal's place is firmly on earth, as a physical being. Animals are to serve, and for this reason the childish attachment to the individual creature must be left behind. *Old Yeller* may appear to be yet another in the tradition of the brave pet movies that were emerging after *Lassie Come Home*, but it is doing something rather different. There is a real (as opposed to fictional) relation to the animal, this film seems to say, and it is always as well to keep that real relation firmly in mind. The trained dog may be talented, just as the brave dog may be valuable, but dogs, like all animals, serve, and then they die. That is what an adult has to come to terms with. Angels milking cows in heaven? That's for children. Growing up brings with it a new understanding of animals. To be an adult involves for Freud a kind of arrogance, for Disney a kind of distance. We are constantly fighting against both of these suggestions, and anthropomorphism plays an important part in that fight.

The upsetting of the comfy relation of children and animals that *Old Yeller* presents is continued in the shift from book to screen that takes place between Dick King-Smith's novella, *The Sheep-Pig* (1983) and Chris Noonan's film *Babe* (1995). In this film something much more terrifying than a sweet tale of a talented piglet emerges. This is achieved in two ways: through the techniques used in the making of the film, and through the content of the film. Together, in telling and story Babe illustrates, I think, the logical conclusion of the dangers of anthropomorphism, and it is not a happy tale.

Goodbye Mom

Dick King-Smith's novella *The Sheep-Pig* tells the tale of Babe, a piglet won in a fairground competition by monosyllabic sheep farmer Hogget. The piglet comes to the farm to be fattened up for Christmas, when, under the guidance of Fly, the sheep-dog, and Ma, the ewe, he learns the art of shep-herding. Farmer Hogget recognizes the skill of his pig, it is saved from the slaughter and goes on to win the Grand Challenge Sheep Dog Trials. In *Charlotte's Web* E. B. White presented his readers with a farmyard full of conversation, and the same is true of *The Sheep-Pig*. But where White had Fern as the only human able to understand the language of the animals, King-Smith does not offer such a human translator. Rather, like *The Wind in the Willows*, we, the readers, merely accept the possibility of these speak-ing animals as we overhear their conversations. However, unlike both Grahame's and White's stories, *The Sheep-Pig* does offer a sense of differ-ence between human and animal that is simultaneously clearly in place – no human ever understands the animals' conversation – but also absent. In *The Sheep-Pig* Farmer Hogget becomes the ideal human: he does not comprehend the animals' conversations, and yet he fully understands the animals. When Fly barks he comes to see what the trouble is, and when Babe begins to show a comprehension of the work of a sheep-dog by herd-ing and separating the ducks, he recognizes this development and encourages it. It is Hogget's ability to transcend the boundary that sepa-rates him from his pig that is one of the most moving things in the story. Here is the farmer, the man of the soil, clearly in touch with his animals in a way that, the book seems to say, no non-farmer can ever be. Even his very talkative wife has no comprehension of the activities of the farmyard until she witnesses the 'miracle' of the sheep-pig on television.

The novel, then, tells a simple story that nods towards discussions of inclusivity (all animals can converse with each other, whatever the species), the need for good manners (Babe wins sheep over through his politeness), the importance of merit (a pig can be a sheep-dog if it can herd sheep, it should not be limited by its species), and, most tellingly, of acceptance. The apparently innate hatred of dogs for sheep, and sheep for dogs, is shown to be based upon a complete lack of understanding on the part of both species. When sheep-worriers kill Ma, Babe is the prime suspect, and Fly asks the surviving sheep what happened, hoping to clear her adopted son. The dog regards this engagement in conversation with sheep as a lowering of her own status: sheep, she thinks, 'were there to be ordered about, like soldiers, and, like soldiers, never to answer back'.[26] Then the sheep tell her of Babe's bravery (he actually chased the guilty dogs away), and the dog comes to realize that perceptions of difference are overblown, and that a dog can communicate with a sheep. Only habit has made it seem impossible.

The relationship between the sheep-dog and the sheep in the book is, I think, parallel to the relationship between humans and animals in the wider world. It might look like stewardship – shepherding – but it is premised upon a rigid belief in the superiority of one species over another; it is a relationship based on dominion. It is with the arrival of the animal that crosses the boundary between dog and pig that other boundaries can be destroyed, the most notable of which is the division between human and animal, and this division is represented through language. At the end of the story, when Farmer Hogget and Babe get full marks in the sheep-dog trials, the world is full of noise – from Mrs Hogget watching it on television at home, from the sheep-pen, from the crowd. King-Smith writes, 'In the hubbub of noise and excitement, two figures stood silently side by side.' The silence is broken by true words from the monosyllabic farmer, '"That'll do," said Farmer Hogget to his sheep-pig. "That'll do."'[27] Saying nothing, but saying everything, the farmer and the pig are an image of a perfect relationship between human and animal; the words are few, mean little, but speak volumes. *The Sheep-Pig* is, in many ways, a grown-up's *Charlotte's Web*: here it is an adult who communicates with animals, not through anthropomorphism but through understanding.

Many of the magical qualities of King-Smith's book are carried through into Chris Noonan's film, *Babe*. Filmed in the countryside of New South Wales, Australia, the farm looks too fantastically lush, the hills too hilly to be true, and so when the apparently real animals begin to speak to each other we know that we are once again in the world of magic realism.

The film, using animatronics and computer-generated animals to achieve its effects, combines the realism of a live action film like *Old Yeller* and the animator's ability to portray speaking animals. Inevitably, however, it is the realism that wins out, and the power of *Babe* is found in the utter believ-ability of the speaking animals. For an audience brought up on *The Wind in the Willows*, *Charlotte's Web* and a menagerie of other animal books, the sight of a 'real' piglet speaking to a 'real' sheep-dog seems to come as no surprise: it is what we have be brought up to believe in. The complex tech-nology of the film, which contains '130 animatronic shots and 130 CG [computer-generated] shots'[28] is hidden by our acceptance of the possibil-ity of speaking animals, and by a certain pleasure in seeing our dreams come to life.

In this sense *Babe* represents the expansion of the empire of the human. No longer limited by the real animal – Lassie could only be trained to look like she was praying, she could never be trained to really pray – new techniques allow us to scan and refigure the real animal to make it do exactly what we please. We no longer have to spend hours training a live pig, we can merely make a robotic one. 'No animals were harmed in the making of this film' may soon become 'no animals were used in the making of this film', and so another ethical dilemma dies away. It's rather like fake fur.

Inevitably such an interpretation of *Babe* only takes us so far. The extraordinary realism of the animals is undoubtedly a cinematic break-through, and reinforces Jonathan Burt's argument that animals have always been central to developments in film technology. But the realism also has another effect. Where it might seem that we are once again putting words into animals' mouths, the human control of the natural world encapsulated in *Babe* soon falls apart. Some key additions to the narrative of *The Sheep-Pig* begin to undercut the cosiness of the book. In fact, the dream-fulfilment at the heart of the book becomes, in the film, a nightmare.

The film opens with a scene of a sow giving suck to her piglets. The chaotic, natural skirmishing of the young animals plays into the world created in natural history films. We get a close-up we have seen many times before on television. But then, a voice-over intervenes to tell us that these piglets live 'in a cruel and sunless world', and we witness the mothers being taken by men from their young, and being replaced with a metal udder that descends from the sky. A piglet peers through the bars of his cage as his mother is driven away, and speaks: 'Goodbye Mom.' This is a phrase that bids farewell to childhood in the film. We have simultaneously the world of natural history films, children's fantasies and industrial farming, and by bringing these together the film-makers add a truly disturbing dimension to the story. Realism and magic realism confront each other and somehow the true magic of the world of the child is gone. The fantasy of the speaking animal begins with a recognition of the horrors of the place of the animal in a human world. The mother-child relation is torn apart. This is not just fantasy, it is not just farming, it is genocide.

We want animals to speak – that is an overriding desire that many of us share – and yet a speaking animal could be a very disturbing thing. Writing in the early twentieth century, the philosopher Ludwig Wittgenstein offered a problem for the fantasy of the speaking animal. He wrote, 'if a lion could talk, we would not understand him'. So different are we from a lion that, even with a shared language, any communication is impossible. Stephen Budiansky has offered a different problem with the same solution. Using Wittgenstein as his model he argues, 'if a lion could talk, we probably could understand him. He just wouldn't be a lion any more; or rather, his mind would no longer be a lion's mind.'[29] Caught between animals who say nothing, and non-animals who say something, the saying something (something that we have created) would appear to be preferable, and yet a speaking animal can upset all kinds of assumptions by saying something we don't want to hear. Anthropomorphism can have an ethical dimension.

On the surface *Babe* is the sweet fantasy of a pig who is good at herding sheep. Underneath this, however, lurks a world of horror, and it is a horror made by humans. On Hogget's farm lives Ferdinand, a duck who has taken to crowing in the morning. This duck on one level is a comic ancestor of the smoking dog: it is an animal performing the wrong function, and is funny for it. But his misappropriation of the rooster's task is for a very good reason: 'Humans,' he says, 'eat ducks.' To crow like a rooster is to be a rooster, is to have a function. The only alternative function available to Ferdinand is as duck *à l'orange*. The appearance in the farmhouse of an alarm clock upsets the fragile stability in Ferdinand's life, and, as the voice-over says, 'The alarm clock had to go. His very life depended on it.' On one level this seems a melodramatic response to the arrival of an alarm clock, and the film certainly plays with a kind of faux *Mission Impossible* theme as Babe attempts to steal the clock without waking the evil house-cat. On another level, however, the duck's desire to steal the clock resonates with a real horror. This duck – who has a name and can speak – is threatened with slaughter, and is attempting to save himself. Realism and magic realism collide, and the film confronts our use of animals head-on. You want to understand their thoughts? it seems to ask. Well, here they are, and they are not pretty. In the light of Ferdinand's struggle to survive, Wittgenstein's solution seems much more comforting. We don't want to know what these animals are thinking, because it is eminently possible that they are thinking about us.

Babe just backs away from the logical conclusion of this story. With the invasion of the human space by piglet and duck discovered, it looks like one or both of them is for the chop. But Babe survives by saving the sheep from thieves, and Ferdinand goes into hiding, ironically, in the slaughterhouse. The fragility of the animals' place in this all too human world is re-emphasized, however, by the arrival of the human family for the festive season. 'Christmas,' Ferdinand notes, 'means carnage.' What is a celebration to us is a massacre to them. Pork or duck is the choice on Hogget's farm, and duck is the selection. For a few seconds we watch, through the window, positioned with the animals, as the Hoggets tuck into duck *à l'orange*. For a moment we are outside of the human world and we confront the horrible possibility that this is Ferdinand's fate. Then, in true comic fashion, the duck himself turns up to have a look through the window. It is not Ferdinand but poor Roseanne, a nice duck we have never met, who is being eaten. We don't know her, so the potential power of the scene is diluted. The film-makers' refusal to represent the consumption of one of the central characters reveals a kind of fear at the heart of even this very challenging movie. To suggest that meat-eating is a form of cannibalism is one thing, to represent it is quite another.

The power of *Babe*, then, lies in a combination of factors. The use of animatronics and computer-generated images combines with a disturbing new storyline and what emerges is a film that is simultaneously sweet and shocking. Anthropomorphism ceases to be sentimental (although the piglet is very cute), it becomes threatening and our fantasies turn into a nightmare. What has happened since the appearance of *Babe* is that the use of animatronics and computer generated animals in film has gone even further. In *Cats and Dogs* (2001), for example, we see a film full of animals with nothing interesting to say about animals at all. Where in *Babe* the *Mission Impossible* moment is a wonderful comic addition to the story, *Cats and Dogs* has nothing but *Mission Impossible* moments (although there is also a bit of *Lassie Come Home* in there as well). In the more recent film, animals are a way of re-using a story that has been told many times before. Animals are new bodies on which to hang old clothes and very little more. It is as if there is a limit to the use of anthropomorphism. On the one side there is a bridge that takes us from animal to human, but on the other it moves us from realism to cartoon. Kung-fu cats have no place in reality, even in our dream reality, whereas a speaking pig does. This is why *Cats and Dogs* fails as an animal film. It has nothing to tell us except to restate the myth that cats hate dogs, and we knew that anyway.

Just as the use of animatronics in *Cats and Dogs* cancels out the animals altogether, so one of the great discussions of animals and machines in philosophy also did some cancelling work with regards to non-humans. In a shift from cinema to laboratory I want to maintain a focus on anthropomorphism. It may seem quite a leap to make but at the heart of both discourses – of fantasy and science – lies one key debate, a debate that continues to rear its head almost 400 years after its first appearance. What is the difference between an animal and a machine that looks like an animal? For film-makers, it would seem, the answer is that there isn't one. For René Descartes, writing over 350 years ago, the answer was the same. The implication, however, was exactly the opposite of what Chris Noonan might have achieved in *Babe*.

The Beast-Machine

In the medieval period, natural philosophy (as 'science' was then termed) looked very different from contemporary ideas about the scientific. Bestiaries, collections of medieval animal lore, presented their subjects not as specimens of the natural world, but as exemplars of morality. One twelfth-century bestiary offers this description of the weasel:

> Some say that they conceive through the ear and give birth through the mouth, while, on the other hand, others declare that they conceive by the mouth and give birth by the ear.
>
> Weasels are said to be so skilled in medicine that, if by any chance their babies are killed, they can make them come alive again if they can get them home.
>
> Now these creatures signify not a few of you fellows, who willingly accept by ear the seed of God's word, but who, shackled by the

love of earthly things, put it away in the wrong place and dissimulate what you hear.[30]

The kind of observation that we take for granted is missing here, and the weasel's alleged method of reproduction is used as a way of speaking not about the weasel as such, but about the human. Like the fables, bestiaries tell us more about ourselves than about the animals, but it is through animals that we learn.

The moralistic modes of medieval science continued to hold power until the sixteenth century when the seeds of what was to become the New Science were sown in the work of men like William Turner and Conrad Gesner. These naturalists combined observation with some of the fables of the medieval world; they recognized that the world around us must be understood as it is, not as it is mythically perceived to be. This sounds obvious to us, with our stereotype of the white-coated scientist experimenting and experimenting in order to find out the 'truth', but the modes of understanding that we assume to be the only ones possible have an origin. The emergence of more modern concepts of science can be seen most clearly in the work of two key figures of early modern thought: Sir Francis Bacon and René Descartes. Both of these men, in different ways, changed the ways in which science was understood and, most importantly in the context of this book, they both had a fundamental impact on the ways in which we live with and think about animals.

Bacon was a statesman working in the courts of Elizabeth I and James I when he became a figurehead in the transformation of natural philosophy. What was central to Bacon's technique was the belief in experimentation: the belief that to find the 'truth' of something it must be observed. In previous centuries classical writers such as Aristotle were regarded as oracles of truth: 'Aristotle says' was a kind of shorthand truth-claim in the works of medieval writers like Albertus Magnus and Bartholomeus Anglicus. Bacon challenged this reliance upon authority and stated 'generally speaking science is to be sought from the light of nature, not from the darkness of antiquity'.[31] We need to see with our own eyes to be able to make scientific judgement. Relying on the judgement of others, even Aristotle, was inadequate for this New Science.

Bacon believed that the emergence of the New Science, this new way of looking at and understanding the world, would increase the power of humanity. Where in Genesis the animals had become wild as a part of God's punishment of Adam and Eve, through science we could, Bacon argued, return to the absolute original form of dominion. Science would be, he wrote, a 'restitution and reinvesting (in great part) to man of the sovereignty and power . . . which he had in his first state of creation'. In a parenthesis – omitted from the previous quotation – he directly likened the understanding of the natural world that would come through scientific endeavours to a return to Eden: 'for whensoever he shall be able to call the creatures by their true names he shall again command them'. Where Adam exercised control through naming, Bacon's follower could exercise it through science. Where we see science as a predominantly worldly, secular concern, Bacon and his seventeenth-century followers regarded it as an extension of their faith. Bacon wrote, 'a little natural philosophy inclineth the mind to atheism, but a further proceeding bringeth the mind back to religion'.[32]

By the 1660s Bacon's philosophy had been institutionalized by the newly formed Royal Society, and the impact on animals is made clear in Samuel Pepys' reports of his attendance at the Society's meetings. In his diary entry for 16 May 1664 Pepys wrote:

> By and by we to see an experiment of killing a dog by letting opium into his hind leg. [Mr Pierce] and Dr Clarke did fail mightily in hitting the vein, and in effect did not do the business after many trials: but with the little they got in, the dog did presently fall asleep and so lay till we cut him up. And a little dog also,

which they put it down his throat; he also staggered first, and then fell asleep, and so continued: whether he recovered or no after I was gone, I know not – but it is a strange and sudden effect.

A similar experiment on the effect of 'the great poison of Moccasso upon a dog' took place ten months later in March 1665, and again in April of that year 'Florence poison' was tried on 'a hen, a dog, and a cat'.[33] Repetition was key. A result achieved only once counted for little, a result achieved every time, repeatable in other laboratories and in the public space of the Royal Society could achieve the status of a fact. This makes many of the scientific books of the time seem something like recipe books. 'You can try this at home' they seem to say, as they explain in detail the experiment. With the right equipment that repetition could easily be done and the emerging facts be confirmed. And repetition, of course, required the use of huge numbers of animals.

The vivisection and dissection of animals has a history going back to at least 500 BC, when Alcmaeon of Croton 'was able to find the function of the optic nerve by cutting through this structure in the living animal and recording the ensuing blindness'.[34] It was in the seventeenth century, however, that experimentation upon animals became absolutely central to the development of science, and that centrality led to an increase in the number of experiments. Dix Harwood argued that developments in science meant that 'animals were butchered ruthlessly in a seventeenth-century version of a Roman holiday'.[35] Where classical Rome had its gladiatorial combats, seventeenth-century Europe had its experiments.

Bacon's scientific philosophy was one of 'induction'. That is, he believed that matters of general truth could be induced from specific instances. Bacon and his followers, then, argued that we can understand the world if we can understand the different individual aspects of the world. The scientist's job is to build up a picture of the world through experimentation and with particular instances. Emerging in continental

Europe was an alternative idea of how the New Science should work, and at the centre of this is the work of René Descartes. He used not the inductive method, but the deductive. Descartes and his followers proposed that we must have a general understanding before we can begin to comprehend individual instances. We need, in short, to begin with the big picture and work down. For Descartes, this was the self. Who is this who is doing the observing? was a question that he put to himself, with the faith that, if he could answer that question he could begin to answer all the other questions that he came across with more clarity. The difference between Bacon and Descartes may seem like a rather abstract one here, but the implications of Descartes's theory had a massive impact upon the ways in which humans perceive animals. As I hope to be able to show, it is an impact that still holds power today.

Descartes looked to himself. In the first of his *Meditations* (1641) he wrote:

> Some years ago I was struck by the large number of falsehoods that I had accepted as true in my childhood, and by the highly doubtful nature of the whole edifice that I had subsequently based on them. I realized that it was necessary, once in the course of my life, to demolish everything completely and start again right from the foundations if I wanted to establish anything at all in the sciences that was stable and likely to last.[36]

Like Bacon he wanted to draw a line through what had gone before, and start from scratch. But unlike Bacon he began with himself. What, he asked, can I truly know to be true, without any doubt? Imagining a demon on his shoulder who would deceive him at every opportunity, Descartes proceeded to doubt all that could be doubted. Do I truly have a body? he asked. His answer, which sounds absurd, was no. We can dream that we exist in a body. When we look at our hands we could be imagining that they are there, and so doubt must creep in. This is 'Cartesian doubt', a central feature of his philosophy. Simply, anything that can be doubted must be dismissed. I can, for example, doubt that I am typing onto my computer right now, because I could actually be dreaming that I am in my office typing. So what is there that cannot be doubted? Simply, my ability to doubt: if I doubt that I am doubting I am, after all, still doubting. From this Descartes came up with his most famous assertion: '*cogito ergo sum*' – 'I think, therefore I am.' My ability to think is the only thing that I cannot doubt, because doubting is a form of thinking.

The implications of Descartes's meditation upon conceptions of truth were massive. A dualism arose that separated mind from body. The body was merely a vessel – a machine, he termed it – in which the self, made up only of mind, was housed. I am my mind, nothing else. So what does this do for the relationship with animals? In his earlier work, *Discourse on Method* (1637), Descartes wrote:

> if any such machines [made by the industry of man], had the organs and outward shape of a monkey or some other animal that lacks reason, we should have no means of knowing that they did not possess entirely the same nature as these animals; whereas, if any such machines bore a resemblance to our bodies and imitated our actions as closely as possible for all practical reasons, we should still have two very certain means of recognizing that they were not real men. The first is that they could never use words, or put together other signs, as we do in order to declare our thoughts to others . . . Secondly, even though such machines might do some things as well as we do them, or perhaps even better, they would inevitably fail in others, which would reveal that they were acting not through understanding but only from the disposition of their organs.[37]

Put simply, for Descartes, animals were machines. They lacked the thing that made a human distinct from an automaton: they lacked mind, and because mind and soul were absolutely inseparable in his thought, animals did not possess souls. Language is evidence of a rational soul, whereas an animal's bark, moo, mew or roar was mere instinct, signifying nothing.

Descartes took his theory of the beast-machine, as his later follower La Mettrie termed it, to its logical conclusion. If an animal is a mere automaton – albeit a wonderful automaton made by the hand of God, a workman skilled beyond any human capacity – then it cannot experience pain. In a letter to Descartes from the philosopher Henry More, written in December 1648, More maintained that Descartes's theory was 'deadly and murderous': 'you snatch away, or rather withhold, life and sense from all animals'. Descartes's defence, written three months later, was clear: belief that animals could think was a prejudice put in place 'from earliest childhood'. Just as in twentieth-century children's literature we have the constant presence of anthropomorphism, so, back in the sixteenth and seventeenth centuries the same ideal of the humanized animal persisted. For Descartes, the dismissal of this childish belief was necessary for the development of a truly scientific philosophy. When we assume that a dog is thinking, are we not in a position to doubt: cannot the smile of an ape not be a smile at all, but a mechanical reaction to external circumstances? Descartes went on:

> I speak of cogitation, not of life or sense; for to no animal do I deny life, inasmuch as that I attribute solely to the heat of the heart; nor do I deny sense in so far as it depends upon the bodily organism. And thus my opinion is not so much cruel to wild beasts as favourable to men, whom it absolves ... of any suspicion of crime, however often they may eat or kill animals.[38]

Just as a clock can tell the time better than a human, and its alarm can be set at an exact time that exceeds the capacity of the human to rouse him or herself without that alarm, so we would never argue that a clock understands that seven o'clock is time to get up. The alarm is merely a mechanical response to an external decision made by the human. In fact, a clock can tell us the time, but it doesn't know the time. An animal, for Descartes, has the same capacity: it lives in the world, responds to the world, but it cannot know the world. Any sign of knowledge that might be shown is mere instinct.

For Sir Kenelm Digby, one of Descartes's earliest supporters, all apparent shows of animal intelligence were based on either instinct or chance, or both. The stealth of the fox, he argued, is not evidence that the fox is stealthy (as a human burglar may be stealthy). Digby argues that the fox's ineffectual chasing of hens leads to tiredness, and the fox 'layeth himself down to rest, with a watchful eye, and perceiving those silly animals to grow bolder and bolder, by their not seeing him stir, he continueth lying still, until some one of them cometh within his reach, and then on a sudden, he springeth up and catcheth her'.[39] This is not the planned cunning of the medieval fox – who the bestiary terms a 'fraudulent and ingenious animal'[40] – this is an instinctive killing machine. The difference is crucial.

The denial of reason to animals that is central to Cartesian philosophy fed into the world of science. The kind of concern shown by Galen in the second century AD, when he refused to use apes in his experimentation on the functions of the brain because of their human-like expression,[41] is lost after Descartes, and vivisection gains a philosophical support. The yelp of a dog is not an expression of pain, it is merely a mechanical response to an external stimuli, on a par with the relationship between a clock and its alarm. The implications of this belief are horrific, and in a parody of the impact of Descartes's ideas, Gabriel Daniel wrote *Voyage to the World of Cartesius* (1692) in which his hero lands in Descartes-world and lives accordingly:

Before my conversion to Cartesianism, I was so pitiful and tender-hearted, that I could not so much as see a chicken killed. But since I was once persuaded that beasts were destitute both of knowledge and sense, scarce a dog in all the town, wherein I was, could escape me for the making anatomical dissections, wherein I myself was operator, without the least inkling of compassion or remorse.[42]

What had been a faith in dominion now became, for some, a scientific fact of nature. Humans are superior to animals; we have a capacity that they lack, and that lack can be used to our benefit. If we need to find out about our bodies, what better place to look than to animals who share the body-machine with us, but lack the senses that might impede experimentation on humans. We should bear in mind when thinking about this early-modern blossoming of vivisection that anaesthetics did not come into use until the nineteenth century, and even then were frequently not used on animals. When a dog was cut open it was a fully conscious dog, experiencing the cut of the knife. But, of course, if that dog could only give an outward show of pain – could howl – and could not really experience pain as we can, then the experiments could go ahead.

It would be overstating the matter to say that all scientists, let alone all people, followed Descartes's line on animals. Many did not, as Henry More's letter shows. In fact only a few took Descartes's ideas to their conclusion on the laboratory slab. But the overriding implication of his work was that humans and animals were physically the same but mentally wholly different. The body – even the human body – is a machine (the heart a pump, joints like hinges and so on) but the human mind is something very special. This is a belief that persists. As Richard Ryder has noted, as a form of self-justification modern-day scientists will still call up a central Cartesian tenet: 'the argument that animals do not feel pain at all, or do so less intensely than humans, is still widely encountered among all those who have a vested interest in inflicting pain'. Ryder goes on, 'when encountered in an intelligent person the motive for this argument can only be deception – of self or other'.[43] In a sense, the division of mind and body allows for what might appear to be one of the great paradoxes of experimentation upon animals. We cut them up, drip solutions in their eyes and so on, in order to tell ourselves about human responses to those same cuts and solutions. That is, in the laboratory the animal body stands in for the human body. This might appear to offer another form of anthropomorphism, where, in place of a Mr Toad exhibiting the fears felt by some humans towards the onset of the machine age, we have a rabbit exhibiting the responses that would be felt by some humans to a new household product like toilet cleaner. The absolute difference between the human and the animal mind, however, means that the testing can remain in place without problematizing human status, or human actions. It becomes acceptable that many experiments that are to our, human, benefit are carried out upon animals that will never feel the benefit of their suffering.

But problems with Cartesian dualism – the separation of mind and body – emerge in experiments upon animals in two ways. In the first are those tests that reveal a difference between the responses of animal and human bodies. In the second are those experiments that are in place to register impact upon consciousness. These areas upset the belief that an animal replicates a human in its physical responses and yet lacks a consciousness that is like the human one, and reveal fundamental flaws in the use of animals in scientific experiments.

In the first case we can turn to what is perhaps the most infamous failure of animal experimentation to 'protect' humans: the case of thalidomide. The drug thalidomide was first used in 1957. It was 'prescribed to pregnant women to combat symptoms associated with morning sickness. When taken during the first trimester of pregnancy, Thalidomide prevented the proper growth of the foetus resulting in horrific birth defects in thousands of children around the world. These children were born in the late 1950s and early 1960s and became known as "Thalidomide babies".[44] The drug had been thoroughly tested on animals, but the results from those experiments and the subsequent deformities in human infants revealed important differences between animal and human responses to the drug. Adverse reactions to the drug were to be found only in humans and 'in a certain strain of rabbit'. Ryder notes that experiments on chickens, hamsters, dogs, cats, rats and monkeys 'failed to produce thalidomide deformities'.[45] The impact of this discovery, and other similar ones, produced a statement in 1980 from The Office of Health Economics (first set up by the British Pharmaceutical Industry in 1962). The statement begins in a way that disturbs all of the certainties that are understood to be central to the place of animal experimentation in modern science: 'the predictive value of studies carried out in animals is uncertain . . . The statutory bodies such as the Committee on Safety of Medicines which require these tests do so largely as an act of faith rather than on hard scientific grounds.'[46] Bacon and Descartes, in different ways, had wanted a science based upon unquestionable fact, upon what could be observed, and not be doubted. The result of some of the ideas that developed out of their work can be shown, three centuries later, to be actually undoing their original desires. Animal experimentation is not science – it cannot prove anything without doubt – it is a place where faith takes over. The faith here is that animals' bodies are the same as humans' bodies, the hard fact of the thalidomide tragedy was that this was just that: faith and not fact.

In the second case where experiments upon animals seem to undo some of the theories that underlie them, we can turn to those experiments on conscious reaction. Richard Ryder records what he terms 'pain research'. 'A Swiss scientist at Sandoz Ltd has researched into pain by immobilizing monkeys in a restraining chair with their heads clamped, and subjecting them to intense electric shock through their tails. He observed "baring of teeth with loud crying, pronounced agitation."' Similarly, 'At University College London, rats were subjected to inescapable electric shock to test the idea that high levels of fear reduce exploratory behaviour.' The conclusion of the researcher is terrifying in its revelation of the pointlessness of the test: 'inescapable adverse stimulation, in this case electric shocks to rats' feet, consistently resulted in subsequent avoidance of the environment in which the shocks had been given'.[47] In other words, the rats stopped going to the place where they were given electric shocks. You don't say.

What is key here, though, is not the pointlessness of the experiments (although that, of course, is important when thinking more generally about animal experimentation), it is the suggestion that these animals' responses are based upon recognizable 'emotions' like pain and fear. Descartes had argued that animals do not possess the reason to experience pain, they merely exhibit physical responses to stimuli that look like the experience of pain. John Cottingham, commenting on some of the paradoxes in Descartes's theory, makes this case in its defence: 'to say that X is in pain . . . is certainly to attribute a conscious state to X; but this need not amount to the full-blooded reflective awareness of pain that is involved in the term *cogitatio* [thinking]'. Animals, he goes on, 'do not have self-consciousness'.[48] A rat's pain is not the same as a human's pain, as a rat cannot fully understand the painfulness of the pain it is experiencing, whereas a human can. In these terms, we appear to have found a philosophical structure to support the continuation of these experiments: there is pain, but at the same time, there is no pain at all, so the animal, by extension, suffers, and doesn't suffer at all. But, of course, if a rat's experience of pain is profoundly different from a human's experience of pain, what is the point of the experiment? The increased knowledge of the rat's experience of pain would seem to be one possible answer, but that question was, in a sense, already answered by the assumption that gave rise to the possibility of the experiment in the first place.

Pain research is also undertaken not for the purposes of learning about behavioural change, but in order to test drugs. Ryder records an experiment in which a scientist 'injected the pain-producing drug bradykinin into the arteries of unanaesthetized white rats'. The problem here, as Ryder sees it, is that 'to induce "writhing behaviour" in a mouse may not be precisely the same thing as inducing pain'. Without language the animal cannot truly tell the scientist what is being experienced, and as such the experiment remains 'inaccurate'. 'One is not studying a visible phenomenon, such as an abscess; one is studying an invisible experience called pain, and the nearest we can get to these experiences in others is through the medium of language.'[49] For accuracy, this experiment should have been carried out on a human subject, but that is deemed unethical. Because of that it is possible, as Ryder does, to question the reason for and validity of these experiments. If it is unethical to test on a human, then the experiment can only be carried out on an animal, but if an animal is not like a human then the experiment is pointless. Such is the logic that is thrown up here.

But, of course, experiments upon animals continue to take place. According to Home Office statistics, the total number of procedures on living animals in the UK in 1999 was 2,656,753, with the total number of animals used 2,569,295. Most frequently used were mice (1,641,868), with 8,185 dogs, 11,684 pigs and a total of 4,003 monkeys also used.[50] With the kind of practical, philosophical and ethical questions that surround animal experimentation, such as the ones that I have outlined above, in place it would seem that either we still adhere to certain assumptions – Christian, Baconian, Cartesian – in which animals are on earth for the advancement of human knowledge and human lives, or we have created an alternative world view. This latter suggestion might be the most terrifying. What might it mean that we know that animals experience the world in ways that are not unlike ours and yet continue to experiment upon them? What does that tell us about ourselves? Animal experimentation seems to provoke this question, but refuses to answer it. It is as if a form of anthropomorphism not unlike that found in children's books, finds its way into the laboratory.

Animals are used because they are like us, but this is a fact that can be read against itself.

The links between human and animal, science and anthropomorphism can be traced in another increasingly important area of contemporary medical research, xenotransplantation. Here, the transplantation of animal organs into human bodies becomes a possibility. As fears about donating and experimentating upon human bodies seem to have come to a head following the child organ scandal at Alder Hey Hospital in Liverpool, so it might appear that animal bodies offer a way forward for medical science. But, as ever, this inclusion of animals in the human world brings with it some serious problems.

Animal-Men

Xenotransplantation is, according to Department of Health terminology, 'the transplantation of tissue and organs between different species, and in particular the transplantation of animal tissue into humans'.[51] The use of animal 'materials' to enhance human health has an ancient history. Medieval bestiaries saw the testicles of the beaver as 'capital medicine' and, writing in the thirteenth century, Albertus Magnus stated that 'haemorrhoids goeth away from him, which sitteth upon the skin of a lion'.[52] But the use of animals not as sources of medicine, but as 'spare parts' for humans brings with it very different problems. In the late seventeenth century a blood transfusion between two dogs was the beginning of attempts to use animals in a new way. In 1666 Robert Boyle wrote of an experiment in which two dogs were placed side by side, and the blood from one transfused into the other until the dog 'donating' his blood was drained dry: it, according to Boyle, 'beg[a]n to cry, and faint, and fall into convulsions, and at last die' by the side of the dog receiving the blood. This experiment was also tried on animals of different species 'as a sheep and a dog, the former emitting the other receiving'.[53]

In June 1667 the experiments went a stage further and, in Paris, the first animal to human transfusion of blood was undertaken. Jean Denis transfused nine ounces of lamb's blood into a human patient that 'apparently cured him of his fever and weakness'. A similar experiment was tried five months later in London when an 'impecunious clergyman', Arthur Coga, was likewise given lamb's blood. One of the experimenters, Edmund King, wrote after the experiment that Coga was 'very sober and quiet, more than before'. A second transfusion pulled in a great crowd, but the experiments were stopped when one of Denis's patients – a madman – died. In France the transfusion experiments were forbidden by magistrates, in England, however, no such ban was put in place.[54]

It was at the beginning of the twentieth century that the first ever animal to human organ transplant was attempted when, in 1906, a pig's kidney was implanted into one woman, and a goat's liver into another by Mathieu Jaboulay. Neither woman survived. Since then experiments have continued, and the world's longest surviving xenotransplant patient lived for nine months with a chimpanzee's kidney in 1963. Subsequently there have been numerous unsuccessful attempts to use animal organs to replace failing human ones. In 1984 two-week-old baby 'Fae' was given a baboon's heart by surgeons at the Loma Linda Medical Center in California. She died after three weeks. As things stand at the moment, it is believed that within two years it will be possible to transplant a pig's heart into a human. These pigs will be genetically engineered humanized pigs, with the introduction of human genes into the porcine foetus intended to help overcome the rejection of the alien organ by the human recipient, and to eradicate possible cross-species infections.

It is this latter issue that is one of the greatest concerns as this new science develops. Many viruses that animals contract might be passed on to humans. This seems obvious. What is not so obvious (and we are back to the kind of problems faced with the different responses to thalidomide here) is that these viruses may not be dangerous to the animals, but might be to humans. Macaque herpes is not fatal to macaque monkeys, for example, but it can kill humans. We are living in a world where it is recognized that 'HIV – the virus that causes aids – may be a Simian Immunodeficiency Virus (SIV) that leapt the species barrier in central Africa'.[55] The lack of knowledge of other potentially species-transferable diseases means that any animals used in xenotransplantation must be thoroughly screened. As the US Food and Drug Administration 'Fact Sheet on Xenotransplantation' notes:

> Animals should be procured from screened, closed herds or colonies that are well-characterized and as free as possible of infectious agents.

> Animals should have documented lineages and be bred and reared in captivity.[56]

The quality of life of these animals will clearly be very different from other animals, but as the current use of pigs' heart valves in human heart surgery shows, animals are already regarded as sources of medical assistance for humans. But the fear of a very real threat to human health that such cross-species transplants might cause remains. One article, published by the Medical Research Modernization Committee (MRMC), states that 'xenotransplantation is a dangerous and unproven technology'. The article goes on to state, 'we must honestly ask ourselves whether we have the wisdom and moral maturity needed to deal with the consequences of xeno-transplantation, and related genetic technologies'.[57] The issue of 'moral maturity' is key, and it returns us to the reason why xenotransplantation is being developed at all. As with everything else, we always turn from animals to look at ourselves.

The Department of Health in the UK, and the Food and Drug Administration in the us both offer the same reason for research into xenotransplantation: lack of human donors. As the FDA factsheet notes: in the US 'between 1990 and 1995, an average of 4,835 people each year donated organs after death . . . Nonetheless, approximately 48,000 people are now on the waiting list for organs, and the number of individuals awaiting kidney transplants continues to grow.' Statistics offered by the British Union for the Abolition of Vivisection (BUAV) show that 'at present only 18 per cent of the UK public carry donor cards'.[58] The need for xenotransplantation, the need to have spare-part pigs, is because of human failures. We are unhealthy: our diets, drinking and smoking, lack of fitness, have meant that we have increased the need for organ transplants ourselves. As the MRMC article notes: 'ironically, it is precisely because people eat too many pigs (and other factory-farmed animals), and have unhealthy lifestyles, that pig organ transplants are being considered'. Not only this, but the low numbers of organ donors means that our unwillingness to allow our bodies to be used to help others after our death creates the need for alternatives. It becomes a kind of terrifying definition of dominion: we cling on to the status of humanity, and turn to animals to plug the holes we make. We are special, they are not: we are individual, they are tools. It should be noted, of course, that it seems that the dualism of Cartesian ideas – the separation of mind from body – that gave a philosophical 'excuse' to experimentation in the first place, is abandoned. Even after death our bodies are considered to be an inseparable aspect of our selfhood.

The obvious alternative to xenotransplantation is a change in the ways in which organ donation is organized. In Belgium, France and Austria 'opt out' schemes exist whereby it is assumed that all are willing to donate organs unless it is specifically stated otherwise. In Austria this has quadrupled organ availability, and in the US it is estimated that up to 75 per cent of the adult population might, with 'presumed consent' in place, become organ donors. It is, perhaps, the general lack of interest in animal welfare within scientific debates that has led to the possibility of a human with the heart of a pig, an irony indeed. We regard animals as tools, the carriers of spare-parts, but we also know that they are enough like us to be able to contemplate using them to patch up our own bodies.

The discussions surrounding xenotransplantation should not be restricted to the medical sphere, however. The ramifications of animal to human transplants can be felt in many other areas of human life: most notably, perhaps, in the imagination. The heart is an emblematic as well as physical object. We know that the beating of the heart pumps blood around the body, but we also conceptualize the heart as a centre of our being. At the sight of the beloved, the heart beats faster; our heart will miss a beat in times of stress and fear; we can be heartbroken. Somehow, the heart is offered as a source of emotions, a source, if you like, of self. If a pig's heart can stand in for a human heart, can fulfil its physical function, does that mean that a pig too can be heartbroken? This would seem to be answered in the affirmative in anthropomorphic children's literature: in *Charlotte's Web*, when the eponymous spider dies E. B. White presents us with a pig in mourning: 'Every day Wilbur would stand and look at the torn, empty web, and a lump would come to his throat.'[59] Likewise in *The Sheep-Pig*, Babe 'felt simply very very sad' after the death of Ma, his sheep friend.[60] The gap between children's book and medical science might appear to be a huge one, but actually the underlying principles of the latter might lead us closer and closer to finding something like a scientific basis for anthropomorphism. The 'humanized' pigs currently being produced as potential xenotransplant donors raise the spectre of the very thing that would make xenotransplantation impossible. Animals are like us, and if they are like us it is very difficult to make the case for using them as if they were like a breathing equivalent of the auto spare-part centre.

The alternative question that might be asked of the affect of xeno-transplantation is, perhaps, even more dangerous. If the heart is regarded as the centre of our emotional being, does that mean that the human recipient of a pig's heart would lose his/her human emotions? For some reason this is virtually unthinkable. It is imaginatively easier for us to transform an animal into a human than it is to transform a human into an animal; we have been raised to believe in the former possibility for centuries.

In the early seventeenth century Francis Bacon wrote, 'infants as they learn to speak necessarily drink in a wretched hotch-potch of traditional error. And however much men . . . advance in wisdom and learning . . . they can never shake off the yoke.'[61] What is imbibed in childhood is impossible to leave behind (Freud, in very different ways, would endorse this). Anthropomorphism has widely been regarded as a thing of childhood, of the time when we lack arrogance towards animals. It is possible, however, to see that somewhere, lurking in the darkest reaches of our so-called adult lives, anthropomorphism still persists. In fact, it might be that anthropomorphism lies at the heart of the very thing that Bacon thought would take us from infancy to adulthood: science.

But there is a possible response to this humanizing of animals that can be traced in even scientific writing. In order to avoid the possibility of regarding an animal like a human we regard animals like objects, without feeling or value. If animals are disposable objects then it is possible to continue to regard them not as fellow-creatures with whom we might want to converse, but as tools for our use. If terms like 'debarking' can be used to describe the removal of the animal's vocal chords, and if a dead cat can be termed a 'mammalian preparation', then the reality of the experiment is lost.[62] What is also lost in this worldview is, of course, what Bacon thought should be abandoned: childish things. Speaking to animals is a fantasy to be put away, subjecting them apparently the adult alternative. In this way *Old Yeller* becomes a truly significant bridge between fantasy and reality, between childhood and adulthood.

The shift from anthropomorph to object can be seen in a comparison of two images. The first is the one with which I began this chapter: Francis Barraud's painting of Nipper, listening. The second is the photograph of the unnamed mouse at the University of Massachusetts Medical School (see opposite). This mouse had the scaffold of a human ear and human

cartilage cells implanted on its back. This is not xenotransplantation, the mouse is merely the host for the ear, and will remain healthy after the ear is removed. The director of this research, Dr Charles Vacanti, claims that this could be a breakthrough in plastic surgery.

Why should these two images be read together? Clearly they are very different: one an oil painting, the other a photograph; one created for aesthetic enjoyment, the other for information. Together, though, the images offer us two of the ways in which we currently think about and live with animals. In the first we have anthropomorphic possibilities – this dog is listening. In the second we have the absolute antithesis. The mouse is not listening, it is not, as far as we can tell, hearing. It is merely an ear. From subject to object, fellow being to tool, animals play their parts in a very confused and confusing world of humans. But there is an alternative reading: Nipper is listening for his master, he is enacting the dream of dominion, a dream premised on the belief in the absolute difference of human and animal. The mouse, on the other hand, is 'hosting' the human, is showing the possibility of a link between the species. This paradox of same and different plays into the fears and delights in all of our relationships with animals.

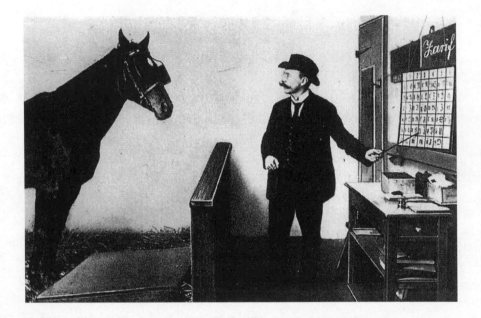

CHAPTER THREE

Intelligence and Instinct: Questions of Power

Can an animal really be taught like a child can be taught? In the late nine-teenth century Karl Krall, 'the celebrated master of the celebrated Elberfeld horses' thought so.[1] He 'taught' two Arab stallions, Zarif and Muhammed, to perform complex mathematical equations (see opposite). He believed, as Jan Bondeson writes, that these horses 'possessed a superior intelli-gence',[2] he thought that they were truly gifted. Their gifts seemed to surpass even those of school children, the training methods for whom (with the notable addition of blinkers) Krall appears to have borrowed. He proposed that 'the horses [could] respond to questions posed in French and Greek (i.e., languages they were never "taught") as reliably as they did to those posed in German'.[3] Mathematical, innately multilingual, these horses were truly impressive.

In 1900 Wilhelm Von Osten, a retired school master, bought an Arab stallion (who was later inherited by Karl Krall), and, for two years, trained this horse to respond to questions with a nod, or a shake of the head, and to perform fairly complex mathematical calculations, tapping out the answers with his foreleg. But Clever Hans, as the horse became known, was not only a fairground attraction. Von Osten was attempting to make a serious point about animal intelligence, and with Hans he felt he had come some way towards proving his case. Clever Hans, it seems, truly was clever.

Psychologists became interested in this horse. How, they wanted to know, did this horse always tap out the correct solution to the mathematical problem he was set? Could it be that this horse really could count? Carl Stumpf, the Director of the Psychological Institute of the University of Berlin was intrigued, and one of his students, Oskar Pfungst, was sent to investigate. What Pfungst discovered was that if the horse was asked a question to which the questioner did not know the answer, then it would get the answer wrong; that its answers were never answers at all. This was a solution that had been offered 300 years earlier to the problem of another intelligent horse, Morocco.

Morocco performed with his master, Bankes, in London in the late sixteenth and early seventeenth century. He could, Thomas Nashe wrote in 1596, distinguish 'a Spaniard from an Englishman'. According to Richard Brathwaite, the horse could 'know an honest woman from a whore', and could, apparently, dance and return a glove to its rightful owner. The poet Joseph Hall wrote of 'strange Morocco's dumb arithmetic': he could count the spots on a dice by stamping out his answers with his hoof.[4] Early-modern explanations for the horse's behaviour varied. Some commentators insisted on the influence of magic, while others regarded Morocco as merely well trained. 'Be wise', Gervase Markham advises, in his early seventeenth-century horse training manual, is a phrase that should warn the horse against incorrect actions.[5] Wisdom, it might appear, is not only the realm of the human.

The similarities between Morocco and Clever Hans do not only lie in their performances. The solution to the 'problem' of both was the same. In 1614, Samuel Rid wrote of Morocco:

his master will ask him 'how many people there are in the room?' The horse will paw with his foot so many times as there are people: and mark, the eye of the horse is always upon his master. And as his master moves, so goes he or stands still, as he is brought to it at the first: as for example, his master will throw out three dice, and will bid his horse tell how many you or he have thrown, then the horse paws with his foot while the master stands stone still. Then when his master sees he hath pawed so many as the dice shows itself, then he lifts up his shoulders and stirs a little. Then he bids him tell what is on the second die, and then on the third die, which the horse will do accordingly, still pawing with his foot until his master sees he hath pawed enough, and then stirs: which the horse marking, will stay and leave pawing. And note, that the horse will paw an hundred times together, until he sees his master stir. And note also that nothing can be done, but his master must first know, and then his master knowing, the horse is ruled by him by signs. This if you mark at any time you shall plainly perceive.[6]

Unlike Bankes's conscious signs to Morocco, however, Von Osten was not aware that he was sending out tiny physical signals that Clever Hans was picking up. So, if asked what five plus eight equalled, Clever Hans would begin tapping the ground with his foreleg, and, when he reached thirteen would recognize an inadvertent, and almost undetectable movement from his owner. It was as if Von Osten would tense up when the horse reached the correct number of taps, fearing, perhaps, that the horse might carry on tapping and give the wrong answer. As Stephen Budiansky has noted, Von Osten 'was no perpetrator of hoaxes but an honest man who firmly believed in his horse's mastery of his subjects'. What seemed like equine intelligence was proved to be merely a response to a previously unrecognized cue. Clever Hans, like Morocco before him, and like many other fairground 'intelligent beasts', was merely responding to his master's body language. He was never really a mathematician at all.

The case of Clever Hans has become, to use Budiansky's phrase, 'a staple cautionary tale in animal behavior research'.[7] What seems like intelligence can often be something else, something we might term instinctive, that even the researcher is unaware of. Von Osten's desire to find intelligence in Clever Hans led him to overlook alternative interpretations of what was going on. The fear of repeating this is one that haunts animal behaviour research, and is one that returns in the case of Nim Chimpsky, which we will encounter later in this chapter.

But, of course, the fact that Clever Hans can't count should not take away from what the horse could do. The cues that he was picking up were tiny – even the person giving them was unaware that they were sending them. To be able to pick up such cues must, in itself, be regarded as a skill, one that Oskar Pfungst had to learn during his research. As Clifford Wilson has noted, Clever Hans's 'truly remarkable ability was in the area of observing rather than of reasoning'.[8] But, of course, observational skills, while important, are never used as a way of distinguishing human from animal. Thinking, or the ability to use abstract reason, is the key to the difference: as Descartes wrote, 'I think, therefore I am.'

This chapter looks at a variety of the ways in which research into and use of animals deals with questions of intelligence and reason, and how the search for intelligence is inseparable from an assertion of human power and dominion. Beginning with work on primate language, and moving through primatology, this chapter also confronts hunting with dogs, and looks at the perception of the fox in hunting rhetoric. If intelligence can be proved (a problematic idea in itself) then wouldn't our attitudes towards animals have to change? A number of problems emerge here. First, animals can be seen to have an intelligence if not equivalent to, then at least similar to, humans, but this does not automatically create change. In the case of fox hunting, in fact, it provides the grounds for a continuation of what can only be described as a deeply anthropocentric activity. Second, our ways of testing for intelligence in animals reveal a cognitive limitation on the part of humans. What comes under scrutiny in all of the aspects of our relationships with animals addressed in this chapter is not so much animal intelligence, but the categories that we use to define ourselves and our animal others, the ways in which we organize our power.

Signs of Life

Language has often been regarded as the domain of the human: that is, a kind of logic can be used that defines the difference between human and animal via the ability to communicate through language. 'I can speak, therefore I am human: it cannot speak, therefore it is not human,' this logic would go, and what follows from such logic is a structure of power. This use of language as a way of differentiating human from animal has a long history, one that brings together discussions of reason and communication. As Richard Sorabji has shown, in Ancient Greek thought 'the same word *logos* could be used equally for speech or reason'. But classical and medieval philosophers did not rest on this simple representation of animals' lack of language to make their case for the human as the only rational animal. A clarification of the terms of the argument was offered, clarification that had the effect of marking even more clearly the gap between humans and non-humans, and of voicing more emphatically human power. Clearly, philosophers such as Aristotle argued, animals can communicate with each other, or as Sorabji puts it, they can 'make meaningful sounds'. However, the sounds they make are not words as such, and therefore animals do not have speech.

The parrot was often offered as a way of making the case against animal language. On one level parrots could speak, and on another they could only make sounds of words, they could not understand their meaning. Sorabji retells the ancient story of Apsethos, 'who taught his caged parrots to say "Apsethos is a god", and then released them all over Libya. The ruse was spotted by a wily Greek who recaptured some parrots and taught them to say, "Apsethos shut us up and compelled us to say 'Apsethos is a god"'.'[9] This distinction between speaking and understanding was crucial. For the medieval philosopher Albertus Magnus, it was necessary to make a distinction between *sonus*, *vox* and *sermo*, that is, between sound, voice and articulate speech. He argued that 'while [some] animals . . . certainly have the capacity to make sound [*sonus*] and may even produce *vox* – sounds signifying to one another some interior state or *affectus* [affection] such as grief, joy, or fear – not all have the capacity to express concepts through articulate speech [*sermo*]'.[10] It is this latter capacity that is regarded as the most important, and, almost inevitably, it is the realm of the human.

Four centuries after Albertus Magnus, René Descartes made what is perhaps the most powerful statement of difference concerning language use. Where the Greeks could use the same term to refer to language and reason, Descartes argued that language was evidence of reason, and that because animals could not speak it is proved 'not merely that the beasts have less reason than men, but that they have no reason at all'.[11] Not noise, not the ability to communicate, but the ability to communicate through language is what distinguishes human from animal. With this powerful philosophical argument in mind, experiments on the possibility of animals learning to communicate with humans through different types of language – sign language, symbolic language – were clearly looking not only at animal capability, but also at the border between animals and humans. If a chimpanzee can be said to 'speak' using his hands, where does the difference between the species lie? Where is our power then?

Experiments to assess the possibility of animals gaining access to human language have taken place throughout the last century. In 1916 W. H. Furness claimed that he had taught an orang-utan to say 'papa' and 'cup', and in 1951 Hayes and Hayes attempted to teach a chimpanzee, Viki, to speak. By the late 1960s, however, a move away from attempts to teach animals to speak was witnessed in the seminal work of R. Allen Gardner and Beatrice T. Gardner. Rather than work with the limited vocal capabilities of a chimpanzee, the Gardners opted instead to use sign language. In their important article published in the journal *Science* in August 1969, the Gardners outlined their work: 'in June 1966,' they wrote, '[we] began training an infant female chimpanzee, named Washoe, to use the gestural language of the deaf.' Washoe, named after 'Washoe County, the home of the University of Nevada', was a female chimpanzee aged between eight and fourteen months when she arrived at the Gardners' laboratory. She had been captured in the wild. The Gardners decided that she should be exposed to as little spoken language as possible, and that communication with her should be through ASL (American Sign Language). 'We wanted Washoe not only to ask for objects but to answer questions about them and also to ask us questions. We wanted to develop behavior that could be described as conversation.' The early signs were hopeful: parents of deaf children confirmed that Washoe's 'variant' use of signs (that is, her improvization with established signs) was like that they witnessed from their own (human) children. Further evidence seemed to come ten months into the project when Washoe pointed to a mug full of toothbrushes in the Gardners' bathroom and made the sign 'toothbrush'. The brushes were 'well within her reach', and, the Gardners concluded, she 'seemed to name an object or an event for no obvious motive other than communication'.

Washoe's vocabulary increased over the following months, and after 21 months she regularly used 34 signs, by the age of five she had 160. These ranged from the naming of objects – flower, blanket, dog, bib – to requests – up, tickle, hurry, please. What impressed the Gardners was Washoe's ability to 'transfer her signs spontaneously to new members of each class of referents'. That is, the sign for 'dog' was not applied only to a specific dog, the dog to which it had originally been applied, but to dogs in general. This gave some evidence that Washoe could shift from the particular to the abstract, that she realized that words did not only refer to their original referents, but could be used to refer to a wider world of objects as yet unknown by the signer. She also began to put words together; 'gimme tickle' was a favourite, alongside other combinations such as 'listen eat' at the sound of an alarm clock signalling mealtime, and 'listen dog' at the sound of barking by an unseen dog.[12]

As well as communicating to her human carers Washoe also began to use sign language on her own. She was caught on camera, in an area of the building that she should not enter, signing to herself the word 'quiet', and, when running to get to her potty in time, she would signal, again with no obvious communicant, 'hurry'.[13] Just as we mutter to ourselves, so Washoe signed. What was being revealed here? Did the Gardners get a glimpse into the otherwise (to humans) impenetrable interior of this chimpanzee's mind, or was Washoe merely signing as a human infant might repeat noises made to it without understanding their meaning, or as a parrot might declare that 'Apsethos is a god'? The difference between these two possibilities, between communication with the non-human mind, and the realization that the non-human mind is truly different from the human, provided a challenge that a number of psychologists and primatologists accepted.

Different methods were used to test for the animal subject's capacity to communicate. In 1971 David Premack recorded his experiments with a six-year-old female chimpanzee, Sarah, using not ASL but magnetized plastic symbols.[14] Another technique was used by Susan Savage-Rumbaugh and her colleagues. Their subject was Kanzi, a male bonobo, or pygmy chimpanzee, who was taught through observing his teachers point to symbols as they spoke. By learning through observation, Kanzi, it was hoped, would 'spontaneously' realize that the symbols were referential. The spontaneity of Kanzi's acquisition of symbol-language was encouraged by the decision to offer no reward for comprehension. His learning was for the sake of learning and communication, not for the sake of a sweet or nut. What Kanzi learned, then, was, first of all, the spoken English, and then the symbols for that spoken English. Kanzi could comprehend a range of spoken words, and could respond using not speech – which his vocal apparatus was hardly capable of producing – but symbols.

Savage-Rumbaugh records that 'During the first three or four years of his life, Kanzi's comprehension of spoken English appeared to be limited to individual words or to sentences within established routines and schemes. During the fifth year he started to respond to more complex utterances, including novel requests that were complex in character and required the integration of novel meaning across words.' Just as a human child gains understanding as s/he matures, so this bonobo developed his comprehension of communication. As with Washoe, it is the combination of words/symbols that most reveals this animal's growing communicative capacity. At the statement 'Jeannine hid the pine needles in her shirt' Kanzi 'turned around, approached Jeannine (there were several people present), put his hand down the back of her shirt, and retrieved the pine needles.' He was clearly able to recognize that 'the word *Jeannine* functioned as a locative, as the recipient of an action, and as the possessor of a shirt'. This goes beyond, say, 'hug Jeannine' where two known words, hug and Jeannine might be brought together without any really problematic alternative interpretations available; it shows, in fact, that Kanzi could understand meaningful phrases and sentences, rather than just meaningful, but isolated, words. Or, as Savage-Rumbaugh puts it, that his comprehension of words is 'sufficiently sophisticated to suggest that he is processing input in terms of simple syntactical structures'.[15]

Savage-Rumbaugh's argument about Kanzi's understanding of 'simple syntactical structures' is a challenge to the work of Herbert Terrace that, in its turn, radically undermined the findings of the Gardners. Terrace, like the Gardners before him, attempted to teach ASL to a chimpanzee, Nim Chimpsky, named after the linguist Noam Chomsky who had proposed that only humans can use grammar, and therefore make sentences. Terrace's discussion of his experiments with Nim was aptly titled 'Can an Ape Create a Sentence?' What Terrace wanted to do was shift the focus of animal language acquisition experiments from the simple learning of names to the more complex understanding of sentences. This, he felt, would be where truly interesting discoveries could be made about animals. Terrace analysed more than 19,000 of Nim's sign combinations, and it appeared that he had begun to uncover a simple, but grammatical, structure in the way Nim communicated. This ape, it would appear, could create a sentence. However, his analysis of nine hours of videotape of Nim revealed something very different. Like Clever Hans before him, Nim, Terrace discovered, was following the prompts of his teachers: or, as Terrace put it, 'his utterances were often initiated by his teacher's signing and they were often full or partial imitations of his teachers' preceding utterance'. As with Von Osten, none of Nim's teachers were aware of the prompts they were giving, nor were they aware of their pupil's capacity to imitate. Terrace then turned to analyse film of the Gardners' experiments with Washoe, and discovered that each of the multi-sign utterances made by Washoe were preceded by 'a similar utterance or a prompt from her teacher'. What he realized was that this persistence of prompts made it impossible for him to think in terms of sentences. Terrace wrote, 'it is important to keep in mind the lack of a single decisive test to indicate whether a particular sequence of words qualifies as a sentence or whether a particular performance qualifies as an instance of grammatically guided sentence comprehension'.[16] This has remained a shadow hanging over all ape-language research. However, Kanzi's ability to respond appropriately to complex grammatical structures – 'Jeannine hid the pine needles in her shirt' – shows that Terrace may have been wrong, and that animals might be able to comprehend sentences, and by implication, might be taught to 'speak' them, through signs or symbols.

Savage-Rumbaugh's claims about Kanzi's ability to comprehend a syntactical structure stand against what she regards as Terrace's key place in ape language studies: 'for many scientists, [Terrace's work] was the final word on ape language, if for no other reason than that it supported their biases'.[17] It is easier to assume human difference than to have to reassess the possibility of animal capacity, and the emphasis placed on Terrace's work, in Savage-Rumbaugh's view, allows for this easier option to continue. Looking for flaws in the experimental technique hides a more general desire to find no language capacity in animals, and, by extension, to leave humans in their state of splendid isolation. But what if the expectation or desire works in another way? What if the scientist wants to find a capacity for language and therefore finds one? What if the true desire to communicate that can be traced in children's books finds its way into these scientific experiments?

Clearly, one interpretation of Terrace's findings is that Washoe and Nim's teachers wanted their pupils to communicate, and prompted them to appear to be doing so without being aware that they were prompting. But another issue also emerges in the production of data related to the animal's signing. Having seen the signs being made by their pupils, the teachers then looked to make them meaningful and as such recorded them as 'words'. This possibility comes to the fore in the experience of a 'native ASL signer' (as opposed to a researcher who had learned ASL particularly for the purposes of the experiment) brought into the Washoe research team. His log of her signs was much more limited than those of his hearing colleagues. More familiar with ASL, this researcher failed to see Washoe make anywhere near as many signs as his colleagues and noted that 'the hearing people were logging every movement the chimp made as a sign'. To him, however, Washoe's gestures were only occasionally recognizable ASL signs.[18] Again, we are not dealing with a deliberate attempt to create fake data by the other researchers, but with their desire to understand the animal. The non-native ASL speakers 'over-interpreted' Kanzi. This is a problem that emerges again and again in animal language research.

Karl Krall, inevitably, disputed Oskar Pfungst's findings regarding Clever Hans and offered more evidence to support the claim for animal intelligence. But his evidence was deeply flawed: when, for example, one of his horses stamped out the answer '24' to a mathematical problem instead of '42', Krall argued that the horse had 'confused the two digits'. 'It never occurred to [him],' writes Gerd H. Hövelmann, 'that he might question the horse's ability to solve complex arithmetic problems.'[19] We might smile at the naiveté of such an adjustment or excuse, but it is not so far away from our 'interpretations' of our pets. The important difference, perhaps, lies in the context. Looking at your pet and reading what you hope to read is a small-scale domestic over-interpretation, whereas in the discourse of science, looking at your subject and reading what you hope to read is more widely problematic. We can find, I think, similar examples in Francine 'Penny' Patterson's work with Koko the gorilla, but we can also find the gorilla's own answers to the problems.

Beginning in 1972 'Project Koko' is the world's longest running animal language experiment. Koko not only learns sign language from Patterson, she is also the figurehead of The Gorilla Foundation, which hopes to 'bring interspecies communication to the public, in order to save gorillas from extinction, and inspire our children to create a better future for all the great apes'.[20] What might be termed the ethical work of the foundation places the animal language experiments in a very different context to those under-taken by the Gardners, Terrace and Savage-Rumbaugh (in their work ethical issues are present, but not so explicitly). Koko is not merely the subject of a scientific study, she is a personality with a public following supported by a website (www.koko.org) where viewers can watch her at work and play, send her emails, buy merchandise, and provide support for the gorilla welfare activities of the Foundation. In a very real sense, Koko's ability to communicate her mind is offered as a reason to respect that mind. The language experiment is very clearly addressing issues of human power and dominion. In this context it might seem somewhat 'picky' to start to analyse the work that Patterson is doing with Koko, but the very popularity of much of her work – the fact that it reaches beyond the pages of journals of science and psychology – means that more than ever we should take, for example, Koko's internet interviews seriously. Koko's role as a celebrity, in fact, brings to the fore some of the problems that emerge in other studies of animal communication.

Two internet interviews with Koko are, at the moment of writing this, posted on the web: one from April 1998, and the other from summer 2001.[21] In both Penny Patterson 'translates' Koko's signs for the web-reader. Both of the interviewers reveal a desire to come to an understanding of what we might term the 'inner being' of Koko. HaloMyBaby ('the moderator of the chat on aol' in the 1998 interview) and Heidi Benson (interviewer for FreeCityMedia in 2001) both question her about her relation to the abstract realm: her future, dreams, ideas about death. We have shifted away from the emphasis upon objects and actions that impact on the immediate world of Washoe and Nim ('gimme tickle'), and are opening up a possibility of a higher level of communication. This shift from the immediate to the abstract is, I think, completely understandable: the signing gorilla appears to give us, humans, our opportunity to ask, 'what's it like being a gorilla?' We want to know that this animal can do more than merely signal a desire for food; we hope that the answers to our more abstract questions will enrich our (human) lives as well as secure gorilla ones. But the recording of Koko's responses poses problems. The shift of meaning that sometimes takes place between Koko's hands and Patterson's translation returns us to the issue of the teacher's desire to understand, to make sense of his/her pupil.

In the 1998 interview Patterson is asked about the Gorilla Foundation's desire to open a gorilla preserve on the island of Maui, Hawaii. During Patterson's discussion of the aim of the preserve – 'a sanctuary for gorillas . . . [a] place where they would be safe and be able to raise a family' – Koko interrupts with the sign 'fake'. When asked what this means Patterson offers what is, I think, a rather over-interpretive translation: 'She knows that what I'm saying hasn't happened yet . . . So, she's indicating that "fake" is not what she has now, even though I'm talking about it . . .' In the later interview Koko's constant signing of 'nipple' becomes confusing. It is her 'sounds like' sign for 'people', but it comes to stand for a number of things. As Benson notes, 'nipple' emerges as 'a metaphor for the mother-baby relationship, nipple as people, nipple as sexual and positive'. It is never just nipple, as that would make no sense, and what happens is that the sign is interpreted as meaningful within its context; sometimes it 'means' one thing, sometimes another, but it always means something. The meaning is often made by Patterson in the translation.

But these somewhat problematic aspects of Koko's internet chats must be placed alongside some of the other information that this gorilla is able to convey, information that does seem to open up the possibility of a gorilla's 'inner life'. When asked about whether she thinks she will ever have a baby, Koko signs 'I don't see it.' She also begins to make 'happy sounds' as Patterson is discussing the possibility of Koko having 'a family of her own'.[22] Earlier discussions with Koko about death might also begin to raise the possibility of some kind of communication across the species barrier. In December 1984, three days after the death of her kitten on the road, Koko's responses to Patterson's questions are strangely moving:

Patterson: Do you want to talk about your kitty?
Koko: Cry
Patterson: What happened to your kitty?
Koko: Sleep cat.
Patterson: Yes, he's sleeping.
Koko: Koko good.

Michael, Koko's companion, also appeared to give evidence of some kind of 'inner being' that is like that of the human. Signing with Barbara

Weller, Michael described a dream.

Weller: How did you sleep?
Michael: Sleep do pull-out-hair.
Weller: Pull-out-hair?
Michael: Pull-out-hair.
Weller: Bad night? Any dreams? What happened?
Michael: Out teeth sorry.

As a note accompanying this conversation records, dreams of teeth falling out are commonly understood to relate to 'actual loss or fear deep in the sub-conscience [*sic*]'.[23] The gap between the species may be closing.

So, what do these language experiments show us? On the one hand we seem to have some evidence of an interior being that only requires access to language to be expressed. On the other, we have the possibility of prompting, of over-interpreting, of making meaning where none exists. Scientific rigour and popular desire seem to be in competition, and the scientists have to find a way of convincing us of the verity of their discoveries, especially where those discoveries seem to show that an ape can produce a sentence, that Kanzi can find the pine needles, and that Michael dreams.

I want to believe that Koko has an interior life; unfortunately I believe that if she does have one she might not choose to live in the compound in San Francisco. That's the danger. If we could hear them speak, we might not want to hear what they say. But something else also emerges from the animal language research, something that is a repetition of Rowlie's comment to Lassie in Eric Knight's novel. In the 1998 interview with Koko HaloMyBaby states, 'I've heard people say she's not really communicating – I think she's smarter than we are – after all, how many of us can speak Gorilla!' This inversion of the original question, in which 'can animals learn to speak human language?' becomes 'can humans learn to speak animal language?', pulls out from under us the notion of our inbuilt superiority that persists in much of the language research. Why is it that our language is primary? Why not attempt communication in the other direction. If we are so superior, surely we should be able to speak ape?

The existence or lack of human qualities that were the focus of the sign-language experiments are most clearly countered in the attempts to understand animals in the wild. To view the thing-in-itself rather than to train the animal to be other-than-itself seems to be the most obvious way of understanding chimpanzees, gorillas, and their nonhuman cousins. But primatology, as we might broadly term this attempt, has a history that reveals something rather different from what we might assume to be its objective representation of the animals' lives, and it brings with it problems that are central to philosophical debates about human knowledge. It also produces findings that raise difficulties in another zone of the human: culture.

Monkey Business

The term primatology was first introduced into the English language by Theodore Ruch, in his *Bibliographia Primatologica* in 1941. As Donna Haraway has noted, the late arrival of the term ('primate' appeared as a species group in 1758 in the work of Carl Linnaeus) equates to the recent changes in the ways in which nonhuman primates were regarded. 'Before World War II,' Haraway writes, 'primatology was overwhelmingly a laboratory and museum-based affair. As subjects of science, living monkeys and apes were in labs and public or private collections, and dead ones were in cabinets and dioramas in universities and museums.' Haraway has traced the unsettling history of the science of primatology through its emergence from the safari shooting-parties of the early twentieth century to the more recognizable contemporary observation of the animals in their own habitats. At the heart of primate studies is what she terms, following the literary critic Edward Said's work, 'simian orientalism'. By this she means 'that western primatology has been about the construction of the self from the raw material of the other, the appropriation of nature in the production of culture, the ripening of the human from the soil of the animal, the clarity of white from the obscurity of color, the issue of man from the body of woman, the elaboration of gender from the resource of sex, the emergence of mind by the activation of the body'. Far from an objective science, with the scientist 'merely' watching and recording, Haraway's vision of primatology is of a science that is inextricably and historically linked with discourses of colonialism, racism and patriarchy, but also with concepts of the human that remove our 'civilized' species from the 'natural' world of animals. For Robert Yerkes, one of the founding fathers of the subject, primatology mediated, in Haraway's terms, 'between categories of culture and nature. The apes were natural objects redesigned to produce useful knowledge. They had no culture . . . They were unobscured mirrors.' In Yerkes's model, we look at primates in order to see ourselves as we are not, but as we would be had culture not 'interfered'. And while doing this, we reinforce our own status as human by regarding the thing that comes closest, and yet remains wholly different. In this way, while primatology has come, in common parlance, to refer only to the study of nonhuman animals, for Haraway, it is 'about the life history of a taxonomic order that includes people'.[24] We may not be looking at ourselves in primatology (a paradox, as we are, after all, primates), but what we see comes only through our own eyes, and inevitably tells us as much (if not more) about ourselves as it does about our animal others.

The human failure to look beyond itself, to achieve the 'objectivity' so desired in our wish to understand animals, is something that philosophers have been contemplating for years. In the 1870s – to cite just one example – the German philosopher, Friedrich Nietzsche, wrote of human intellect that it 'has no additional mission which would lead it beyond human life.

Rather, it is human, and only its possessor and begetter takes it so solemnly – as though the world's axis turned within it.' His essay, 'Truth and Lies in a Nonmoral Sense' takes human morality as a construct with no relation to actual existence in the world, and human knowledge lies (in both senses of the word) at the heart of his argument. Animals are the obvious blind-spot for Nietzsche's humanity. In the same essay, Nietzsche writes of truth:

> When someone hides something behind a bush and looks for it again in the same place and finds it there as well, there is not much to praise in such seeking and finding. Yet this is how matters stand regarding seeking and finding 'truth' within the realm of reason. If I make up the definition of a mammal, and then, after inspecting a camel, declare 'look, a mammal,' I have indeed brought a truth to light in this way, but it is a truth of limited value. That is to say, it is a thoroughly anthropomorphic truth which contains not a single point which would be 'true in itself' or really and universally valid apart from man. At bottom, what the investigator of such truths is seeking is only the metamorphosis of the world into man.[25]

We see what we are able to see, what we expect to see, what we have already decided to see, rather than what we might call the truth. The same, it seems, could be said of endeavours to understand primates. Primatology seems to be presenting us with animals as they really are – something that is especially the case in the televisual representation of primatological research – but Haraway and Nietzsche, coming from very different angles, would both argue that something else is going on. For Haraway the reality of primatology is bound up with political and social concerns: 'primatology is western discourse, and it is sexualized discourse'.[26] For Nietzsche, the attempt to account for, understand and represent animals would be evidence only of human limitation.

Nietzsche's sense of the inevitability of human limitation is something that is given a comic spin in Will Self's *Great Apes*. In this novel Self creates a world that is a total inversion of reality. Apes live in houses, have jobs, families, walks in the park and so on, while humans live in cages: 'They're so cute' remarks one chimp visitor to the human enclosure at London Zoo. In this narrative primatology becomes anthropology, 'a branch of zoology which had always attracted zealotry' in the world of chimpanzees, and at the end of the novel a group of chimps travel to Tanzania to visit Camp Rauhschutz, the home of the great chimpanzee anthropologist Ludmilla Rauhschutz. One evening, the tourists sit with Rauhschutz and listen to the night-time calls of the rehabilitated humans who roam free in the surrounding forest. 'Fuuuuuuckoooooooffff-Fuuuuuuuckoooooooofff', comes a cry from the forest, to be answered with another 'Fuuuuuuuckoooooofff-Fuuuuuuuckoooooofff.' Rauhschutz is asked 'Did that particular set of calls have any meaning?' 'Yes, it does,' she answers. 'That is the human nesting vocalisation. It's a tender exhortation by the male humans to the females, saying that the night shelters are prepared and it is time for mating activity to begin.'[27] Chimpanzee manners and expectations are transferred onto the humans, and the latter are read as if they were like their observers, or like their observers would want them to be. Difference is collapsed, and what emerges is a similarity that can clearly serve ethical ends ('how can we hurt them when they're so like us?') but that simultaneously obscures what is human about the humans.

Will Self's brief comic indictment of the work of Rauhschutz echoes fears held implicitly, if not explicitly, by the primatologists working in the real world, and a mode of interpretation – ethology – becomes the basis of their work in order to make a distinction between popular (anthropomorphic) and professional (scientific) practices. Ethology is an attempt to comprehend, through observation, recording and comparison, the reality of animals' lives. Unlike behaviourists, who 'focus on a few domesticated animals, such as rats and pigeons, as "models" of the species that we belong to,' ethologists, Frans de Waal argues, 'are interested in animals for their own sake'.[28] The implication here is that ethology 'judges' according to the rules of the animals themselves, not the human observers; that animal behaviour is understood within the context and meaning given to it in the animal's world, not the human's. But this question of objectivity is a difficult one. Real objectivity would deny anything like human activities to animals: calling chimpanzee social structures 'families', for example, would be impossible, as such a term brings with it a host of meanings from certain areas of human culture that are impossible to transfer directly on to animals. Jane Goodall, for example, wrote in 1993: 'When, in the early 1960s, I brazenly used such words as "childhood", "adolescence", "motivation", "excitement" and "mood" I was much criticized. Even worse was my crime of suggesting that chimpanzees had "personalities". I was ascribing human characteristics to nonhuman animals and was thus guilty of that worst of ethological sins – anthropomorphism.'[29] However, and we're back to a problem already faced in this book, if description using human language and human ideas is not possible, what is? How can we fail to see with our own eyes? What alternative do we have? The ethologist Robert Hinde has noted this difficulty, and answered it in pragmatic terms: 'fear of the dangers of anthropomorphism has caused ethologists to neglect many interesting phenomena, and it has become apparent that they could afford a little disciplined indulgence'.[30] Rather than this being an ethical concern, Hinde's acknowledgement that anthropomorphism is inevitably going to have a role to play in ethology is an acceptance, I think, that we can only see what we see; that we can only describe what our language allows us to describe. It is better to (slightly) humanize, this argument seems to go, than to be silent about and ignore animals, and the latter is probably the only real alternative. So, what did the primatologists find when they looked at their subjects? Inevitably, and, for some humans, terrifyingly, they found one of the things that was assumed to be the domain of the human. They found, in fact, culture.

Answers to the question 'what is culture?' have been suggested for centuries. In the mid-nineteenth century Matthew Arnold argued that culture is 'the best that has been thought and said in the world'.[31] It is the realm of poetry, art, philosophy. This limitation of culture to the realm of what we might term 'high culture' – opera, ballet, 'great' literature and so on – still holds some power in our society, but it has been countered by alternative ideas. In 1871 Edward Tylor offered a slightly broader range of possible areas when he proposed that culture is 'that complex whole which includes knowledge, belief, art, law, morals, custom, and any other capabilities and habits acquired by man as a member of society'.[32] 'Man' alone, for Tylor, was the possessor of culture. Into the twentieth century, definitions of the term continued to be offered that seemed to become more general. Raymond Williams, to cite just one, proposed that the term should be broadened in its application: culture, he argues, is 'a whole way of life'. It is something more like the air we breathe than the books we read. It is something that we are always already in, that we do not have to go to a library, an opera house or a church to experience. In Williams's terms, literature, art and so on become just particular – and particularly insightful – elements of culture. They are not, on their own, the thing itself.[33] It is clear that the definition of culture offered by Williams is one that might be of use to those involved in the study of animals. While horse ballet exists, the horses always perform at the behest of the human trainer; ballet is not something innate to the horse.[34] But if culture is a whole way of life, then it would be hard to deny culture to any animal. All animals have 'a way of life', all that we need to do is attempt to understand – albeit with the inevitable limitations of our own perceptions – what that way of life might be.

Frans de Waal offers another definition of what culture might be: he cites the Japanese primatologist Kinji Imanishi's proposal that culture should be defined 'not by technical achievements or value systems, but simply as a form of behavioral transmission that doesn't rest on genetics'.[35] That is, that culture is made up of activities that are not confined to the biological or ecological limitations of the animals' world, but that are passed on from generation to generation. In this sense, culture requires time to be assessed. An activity must be inherited for it to be culture. The shift in definition from Williams's broader sense of 'a whole way of life', to Imanishi's behavioural transmission over time is a significant one for primate studies. The concept of 'behavioural transmission' implies two crucial things. First, that there is a social world in which behaviours can be learned. Second, that there is a history. The assertion that animals have a history – their own history – is an important one. In his *Philosophy of History*, the German philosopher G. W. F. Hegel wrote of Africa; 'it is no historical part of the World; it has no movement or development to exhibit … What we properly understand by Africa is the Unhistorical, Undeveloped Spirit.' To have a history a people must also have a civilization, and, to Hegel, writing in the early nineteenth century, Africa lacked the latter, and therefore the former. Historians since then have been attempting to challenge this understanding, and the racism of the historical tradition that followed from it that regarded much non-Western culture as unimportant, unworthy of analysis.[36] Acknowledging that a group has a history is simultaneously acknowledging that that group has some part to play in the world. Lacking history, in Hegel's terms, means lacking any capacity – reason, maturity – that might designate a group as worthy members of the human community. Imanishi's concept of 'behavioural transmission', then, becomes a very significant one for anyone interested in asserting the possibility of animal culture in that it provides a way of assessing it, even as it gives animal society a past, a present, and, by extension, a future.

One of de Waal's examples of such animal culture is the potato-washing activities of a group of monkeys on Koshima Island in Japan. In September 1953 Imo, an eighteen-month-old juvenile monkey 'carried a sweet potato to a small freshwater stream' and rubbed the soil off of the potato. This action, which would save the monkeys' teeth from wearing down, 'first spread horizontally, from Imo to her playmates. Within three months, two of her peers as well as her mother were showing the same behavior . . . Within five years more than three-quarters of the juveniles and young adults engaged in regular potato washing.' In the almost 50 years since Imo first washed a potato, soiled potatoes have ceased to be available in Japan, and the animals are fed with pre-washed ones, but the activity continues. Now, however, the monkeys 'dip' the potatoes into the shallows of the ocean before taking a bite. The researchers have termed this activity 'seasoning'.[37] These monkeys do not eat merely as a response to a physical hunger, they eat to taste: their food, in the terms of Claude Lévi-Strauss, the great structuralist anthropologist, has crossed the boundary from 'raw' to 'cooked'. It has been transformed from its original state in order to be consumed, something that it is, for Lévi-Strauss, a mark of culture.

Other activities by nonhuman primates have likewise undone the exclusive connection between humans and culture. The manufacture of tools – sticks to pry termites from termite hills, chewed leaves used as sponges to soak up water for drinking – is now commonly recognized in primate studies, and gives evidence that these monkeys and apes are able to manipulate their environment, rather than merely exist in it. In June 1999, a further step was taken. A group of primatologists, including Jane Goodall, proposed not only that chimpanzees had culture, but that 'there is significant cultural variation' between chimpanzee communities. That is, just as there are variations in dress code, manners, gestures and so on in human culture, so such differences exist in ape and monkey culture. 'We find,' this group of primatologists state, 'that 39 different behaviour patterns, including tool usage, grooming and courtship behaviours, are customary or habitual in some communities but are absent in others where ecological explanations have been discounted.'[38] Regional variation offers a picture of an even more complex primate culture. Groups of animals are working to rules that are not instinctive or natural, but that are created, cultural. The language of these animals may not be a spoken language that we can easily translate, but the pant-hoots and purrs are given a new status once the context in which they are 'uttered' is made meaningful. A scream of a chimpanzee may not be an 'articulate utterance' to us, but, to the chimpanzees within its own community, it is. This is a crucial acknowledgement of difference; an acknowledgement that the untranslatability of chimpanzee into human language may not be a failing on their part but a recognition that our (human) language is not Language itself; that we do not have the monopoly on meaning. This is something that also becomes visible in experiments on consciousness in animals, but, again, the story is not a simple one.

Testing Times

How can animal intelligence be tested? Is it possible to find a way to be able to say unequivocally that animals think, that we humans are not the only ones with access to rationality? This is a question that has been answered in a wide range of ways by psychologists, animal behaviourists and zoologists, and evidence does seem to emerge to support a view that would undermine Descartes's assertion that reason is a purely human domain. Marian Stamp Dawkins relates the story of Alex, an African grey parrot trained by Irene Pepperberg at the University of Arizona. Pepperberg 'realized that one of the reasons that most talking birds don't seem to understand what they are saying' – remember 'Apsethos is a god' – 'is that people teach them to speak in ways that make it impossible for them to make the link between the sound of the word and what it stands for'. Alex was, therefore, given a very different introduction to language – using a technique rather like Savage-Rumbaugh's ape language experiments – and he appeared to develop an understanding of differences in shape, colour and number that could be transferred from one group of objects to another. Alex, it would appear, could count, and he even used language to express an opinion. 'It is disconcerting, to say the least,' writes Dawkins, 'to watch videotape of an unsuccessful training session in which a parrot refuses to co-operate with his trainer and then see it terminated by the bird itself moving off-camera muttering the words "I'm going away!"'[39] One is reminded of Washoe's signing of 'quiet' when in the forbidden area of the building.

Other experiments on other animals offer more 'evidence' of conscious thought processes. Lesley J. Rogers outlines an experiment on pigeons using keys with different patterns on them. Three keys are displayed, the centre one has to be matched to one of the others, and the pigeon gets a food reward each time it selects the match. Developments from this original experiment show, Rogers argues, 'that pigeons are remarkably good at solving very complex problems using . . . visual displays on the keys'. Work at the University of Bochum in Germany further developed this understanding of the pigeons' capacity. Juan Delius put 'mental rotation' problems in front of the pigeons. The bird had to match one shape to its twin, displayed among many, but put at the wrong angle. In humans, the rotation of the shape meant that it took longer to identify the twin, whereas in the pigeons, the solution was offered 'just as rapidly' as it had been when the shape was represented at exactly the same angle. Delius proposed that pigeons were 'geniuses in comparison with the humans!' But Rogers offers a rather more nuanced response: 'this may mean that pigeons solve the problem using quite a different cognitive strategy, possibly related to their experience of looking down on objects in a horizontal plane and thus with no preferred angle of orientation'. She adds, crucially, 'their strategy is clearly not an inferior one'.[40]

What the experiment with shapes shows, therefore, is that in the world of the pigeon such activities are undertaken constantly as they are flying, and because of this the results of the experiments reveal an existing propensity to recognize shapes since that is a skill that is necessary to their continued existence. Teaching an ape or a parrot to count, however, brings with it other questions. Hank Davis, who has worked on animal numeracy has argued that 'absolute numerosity is a distinctly human invention. No nonhuman animal needs this form of numerical competence to lead a successful, totally normal life . . . Once again human investigators have taken some characteristic human ability and gone looking for rudiments of it in other species. Certainly, there is an arrogance or anthropocentrism in this activity.'[41] The linguist Noam Chomsky has said something similar about the ape-language experiments: 'If you want to find out about an organism you study what it's good at. If you want to study humans you study language. If you want to study pigeons you study their homing instinct.'[42] What is revealed in ape language and many animal intelligence experiments, Davis and Chomsky argue, is not so much the animals' capacity, or incapacity, as our inability to look beyond our own frames of reference. We judge things on the basis of whether or not they are like us; and they fail on that basis too. This hardly seems a fair contest.

A similar recognition of the important differences between human and animal intelligence has been proposed by Stephen Budiansky. His case is simple. We need to assess animals as animals, not as humans. Chomsky mentioned the pigeon's homing instinct, and this is something that Budiansky also discusses; the pigeon's skill has important implications for our conceptualization of animal intelligence. Pigeons have an internal compass. They perform their astonishing feats of navigation by comparing 'the position of the sun with their internal clocks to determine compass direction'. They may also, Budiansky adds, 'be able to use the earth's magnetic field as a back-up compass on cloudy days'.[43] Where we need maps, satellite navigation systems, passing strangers, pigeons have within themselves everything to get home. We have what might be regarded as cultural artefacts, they have no such thing. The pigeon's homing instinct is just that, it is an instinct, an innate – not learned – capacity. But it is for this reason, perhaps that we do not regard it so highly as a gorilla signing about her kitten, or a parrot refusing, in language, to take part in an experiment.

Both of the latter are things that we might do. Without training, maps, road signs, we could never get home. The pigeon's skill is an alien skill, and is valued differently because of this.

We are surrounded with similar displays of animal skills that we often fail to recognize as just that. The lack of recognition is not because we don't know that pigeons get home somehow, it is because we use our own frame of reference to judge the world around us, and because of this we often fail to see and truly assess much of what happens. Like science, pet ownership and so much more, categories of understanding are constructed through history, not natural, and we should bear this in mind as we attempt to comprehend animals.

In his study of the transformation of the ways in which humans understand and categorize the world around them, the French philosopher Michel Foucault uses as an example the taxonomic scheme in a story by the Argentinian writer Jorge Luis Borges. In the passage that inspired Foucault, Borges represents 'a certain Chinese encyclopedia' that divided animals into categories unrecognizable to contemporary biological sciences. Those categories are: '(a) belonging to the Emperor, (b) embalmed, (c) tame, (d) sucking pigs, (e) sirens, (f) fabulous, (g) stray dogs, (h) included in the present classification, (i) frenzied, (j) innumerable, (k) drawn with a very fine camelhair brush, (l) et cetera, (m) having just broken the water pitcher, (n) that from a long way off look like flies'. Foucault comments, 'In the wonderment of this taxonomy, the thing we apprehend in one great leap, the thing that, by means of this fable, is demonstrated as the exotic charm of another system of thought, is the limitation of our own, the stark impossibility of thinking that.'[44] Classifying on the basis of 'that from a long way off look like flies' is, to us, ridiculous, but only because our categories appear true and natural. But the affect of Borges's work is to lay bare the apparent natural-ness of our classifying systems. The Chinese encyclopedia may make us wonder why, for example, the having, or not having of a backbone – vertebrate, invertebrate – is so central to biological classification. But because of its embeddedness in our system of thinking it seems impossible to overturn it. It is something abnormal that has been normalized. As Nietzsche noted, we see a camel and classify it as a mammal, and are pleased that we have discovered the 'truth'. The fact that we made that truth in the first place, that it is not 'natural' – as in, 'out there' – passes us by.

The way in which the pigeon gets home is like a category in Borges's encyclopedia: it is beyond our realms of classification. As such it is an 'impossibility' for us to think of it as a simple proof of the animal's intelligence. The homing instinct, therefore, fails to enter into our discussions not because it is not an astonishing skill, but because our understanding of what is meant by 'intelligence' excludes things like inbuilt compasses. Intelligence is always something that we can do, or that we can aspire to do. Finding our way home from an unknown place with no external aid might not be, whereas correctly using a map is. We are constantly surrounded by evidence of animal skill, but it is often in places where our category 'intelligence' does not operate: the homing instinct is termed an instinct, not intelligent behaviour. It is as if the pigeon has no choice but to go home, whereas we can choose to get lost.

This skill in animals may not be classed as intelligence, but it is often something that we are happy to use. When police and customs officers rely on dogs to sniff out drugs two things are revealed: first, we are, as humans, incapable of finding the drugs on our own (we fail), and second, the dog has a better sense of smell than us (it succeeds). We do not, however, then go on to shift the ground of the debate about the nature of the reasoning mind to take on this canine success. We simply regard the dog's skill as being a natural capacity, not a form of intelligence at all. If we shifted the concept of intelligence to take in ability to scent, and ability to get home with no map, we might find that we are no longer at the top of the pile. It is only when abstract thought, and a (communicated) sense of self are used as keys to explain intelligent, conscious behaviour that humans emerge on top. On this basis it is little wonder that we won't broaden our notion of intelligence, that we don't change the frame of reference. If we did, everything else would change.

But, of course, there are places in our world where we do acknowledge the existence of intelligence in animals. Beyond anthropomorphism, and in the practical realities of everyday life, there are relationships with animals that are formed on the basis of productive intelligent interaction. In these relationships it is impossible, I think, to offer anything but 'intelligence' as the label for what it is that the animal is displaying. What emerges from a brief look at the training of guide dogs, and the responses to having a dog trained by guide dog users, is a sense of closeness that appears to dismiss the kinds of distinction between human and animal that have been the foundation of many of the experiments discussed so far. The guide dog, in fact, emerges as a truly problematic 'animal'. Acknowledging intelligence in an animal does not, however, automatically bring anthropocentrism to an end, as something like Project Koko might seem to propose. A look at the ways in which hunters perceive their quarry offers evidence of the ways in which we can have the animal as both clever and as the instrument of our pleasure simultaneously.

Myself and My Enemy

Guide dogs were first introduced in Germany in 1916 to aid soldiers blinded in the First World War. An article written about these early guide dogs in 1927 by Dorothy Eustis raised international awareness of the possibilities of using dogs to enable people with impaired vision, and in 1928 The Seeing Eye organization was established in Switzerland and the USA. In Britain, the Guide Dogs for the Blind Association (GDBA) was established in Wallasey in October 1931 by Muriel Crooke and Rosumund Bond, and it has, in its 70 years, trained 21,000 human-dog partnerships.[45] In the

US Guide Dogs for the Blind, Inc. was established in 1942, just after America entered the Second World War. They estimate that they have trained over 7,500 teams since then.[46]

Many of the dogs trained as guide dogs are bred by the training organizations themselves. The ideal guide dog is one who is 'stable; of a happy, pleasing disposition; not neurotic, shy or frightened; reasonably energetic; not hyperactive; not aggressive: pure apprehensive protective; of low chasing instinct. Able to concentrate for long periods. Not easily distracted. Willing,' the list goes on. The GDBA is engaged in crossbreeding to create this ideal; it is 'producing dogs that combine the tolerance of the Labrador with some of the sensitivity of the Golden Retriever'.[47] The 'character' of the dog is crucial to its potential to complete the expensive and strenuous training process: the GDBA estimates that it costs 'around £35,000 to breed, train and support each guide dog'; Guide Dogs of America puts the cost at 'approximately $25,000 or more, which includes the cost of training the dog and providing instruction for the guide dog user'. An early judgment of the animal's potential is vital if vast sums of money are not to be wasted.

Once selected, the dog begins its training with a 'puppy-walker'. This volunteer raises the pup for the first year to fourteen months of its life. Once the animal reaches maturity it leaves the puppy-walker and attends training school. At 'graduation' in Britain the dog receives a white harness in place of its brown training harness, and the new owner pays 50p to take the graduating dog. According to Guide Dogs for the Blind, Inc. there are nine phases of training for the dog to get through. These include the physical examination, preliminary harness training, introduction of distractions, obstacle courses, 'mall exposure' and traffic conditioning.[48] But most important of all is the dog's learning of what is termed 'intelligent disobedience'. That is, the dog must learn when it is necessary to go against the wishes of its blind companion: must, for example, refuse to cross the road when it can see a danger that the human cannot. This is a step further than

Rudd B. Weatherwax went with Lassie. Lassie was trained to do things, guide dogs must be trained not to do the things they are trained to do, and the dog must understand this contradiction. It is impossible not to begin to think in terms of canine judgment. The dog does not merely follow orders, it has to make split-second judgments on those orders. One graduate of the Guide Dogs for the Blind, Inc. in the USA recalls her dog's 'intelligent disobedience':

> I approached a corner and told Parke to go forward. The light had changed and the traffic started. As we stepped off the curb, she stopped, turned around, and pulled me back to the curb. I was coaxing her to behave and cross the street, when the instructor who was with me explained that I should be praising her instead. A bus had turned right in front of us; she took me out of harm's way.[49]

'Intelligent disobedience' is far beyond Clever Hans's reactions to the tiny physical cues of his questioners. These dogs are able to answer questions to which their owners cannot know the answer.

In this sense the dog enables its human companion to live an 'independent' life, but, of course, independence would seem to stand at odds with the real sense of the necessity of the animal. If the dog is not present then there is no autonomy, and yet dependence on the dog paradoxically creates independence. In an article on the impact of guide dogs on the lives of their human companions by Clinton R. Sanders, two of his interviewees answer this apparent contradiction: 'With a dog you are a whole. You are not two people trying to function together, you're one unit. Even though you are two bodies it doesn't feel that way.' 'People ask me if she's my best friend, or if she is more like my child. [My dog] is my eyes. What is your relationship with your eyes?' The skill of these dogs transforms not only the life of the owner, but the nature of the dog itself. As Sanders puts it, 'the dog and person are defined by self and others as a unitary social actor. In this sense the dog is transformed into a literal extension of the owner's self.'[50] Not merely a highly trained appendage of the human, the dog completes what is incomplete, and in doing so becomes a part of the human. Where the assertion of the absence of intelligence in animals would seem to mark out a clear boundary between us and them, the guide dog's intelligent disobedience makes such a boundary impossible. In fact, the boundary between human and dog must be torn down in order for the human to be fully human again.

Not too distant from the thinking behind xenotransplantation, although clearly much more concerned with the long-term welfare of the animal, guide dog training organizations create animals to make up for human lack. Loss of sight, or severe visual impairment, is counteracted, not by human science and technology – although the GDBA does fund research into blindness – but by human-animal interaction, and by animal intelligence. If the dog can become its companion's eyes, then the distance between what a human sees and what a dog sees cannot be too great. We do not have to account for differences like the pigeon's inbuilt compass here, rather we need to think about the possibility of similarity. Anthropomorphism – an often derogatory label applied to ways of seeing animals as if they were the same as humans – might actually be unfairly naming something that is not so human-centric. Maybe animals are more like us than we want to imagine and the label 'anthropomorphism' merely allows us to recognize this and devalue it simultaneously. That is, we sometimes use the term 'anthropomorphism' to undercut the dangerous possibility that the gap between human and animal is not so large after all. Or, maybe we can reverse this; maybe there is something else that we do not want to acknowledge. Annabelle Sabloff kept a diary of her observations of a cat raising her kittens. In this diary she wrote, 'How human this cat mother is!' Later she realized that she 'had put the emphasis in the wrong place. What I came to sense eventually was not how human this cat family was, but rather how catlike human family behaviours are; in other words, how similar are many human and other mammalian interactions.' But this original error was not merely Sabloff's own. It was, she argues, symptomatic of a more general cultural failing. 'My original "inversion" was an example of how we tend to mute the animal in human being. And, along with this Western penchant for ignoring continuities in interspecies behaviour between humans and other animals, we also engage in muting the animal in human beings more actively through ideology and through the adoption of powerful cultural blinders.'[51] The problem that the guide dog poses to the category 'animal' is only a problem because of the category, not because of the dog. We see animals, and we see ourselves, through the categories that we have created, and what doesn't fit is not eccentric, rather it shows how frail our structures of thought are. Maybe animals are like us: maybe we're like them. Perhaps it is our categories themselves that give us our separation?

It would seem, then, that the conceptualization of the fox in hunting discourse would be wholly different from this understanding of the dog in its role as guide. What is needed here, you would imagine, is a clear boundary between humans and animals, a boundary that would allow for unquestioned dominion. The language of the hunt, however, seems to point us in a different direction. Ironically, it might seem, the creature that is the object of the hunt is given a status that would appear to be at odds with the nature of the activity itself. It is a sad fact that a recognition of something like equivalent abilities in an animal does not call a halt to human dominion, in fact, in hunting it seems to promote it.

One of the greatest defences of hunting that can be offered, it would seem, is an appeal to the past. There are two ways of doing this: one mythic the other historic. Roger Scruton proposes the former. 'Planted in us, too deep for memory,' he writes, 'are the instincts of the hunter-gatherer, who differs from his civilized decendants not only in making no distinction between the natural and the artificial order, but also in relating to his own and other species in a herd-like way.' He goes on, 'the experience of the hunter involves a union of opposites – absolute antagonism between individuals resolved through a mystical identity of species'.[52] Like Kenneth Grahame in *The Wind in the Willows*, Scruton uses animals in *On Hunting* to image a way back to a more perfect society. Hunting allows us, he argues, to become truly ourselves again. But the other argument that is often made in defence of hunting, and one Scruton occasionally slips into, has to do with the nation. Hunting with dogs is a part of English heritage, and to lose it would be to lose something noble, wonderful about England. What would the countryside be, this defence seems to ask, without the hunt?

However, the claims for the mythic and/or historic importance of fox hunting, as Tom Regan has noted, merely reveals the close connection to the other convention that is at work in this defence: 'it is', he writes, 'traditional to view animals as mere receptacles or as renewable resources'. He goes on, 'these appeals to tradition, in other words, are themselves symptomatic of an impoverished view of the value animals have in their own right and thus can play no legitimate role in defending a practice that harms them'.[53] By claiming tradition as their shield, huntsmen and women are also claiming a very distinct view of animals, a view that is at odds with changing assumptions that might include issues like the ape language experiments, the importance of guide dogs for the blind and so on. If our inheritance is one in that represents animals are mere objects for our use and pleasure, then that inheritance might be one that is worth giving up.

But, if the huntsmen and women are claiming tradition as their defence it is worth reviewing that 'tradition', because in it we can find an ambivalence that lays bare some of the claims for animal intelligence. In the medieval and early modern periods the fox was always figured as 'vermin', a category that included those animals which, as Mary Fissell has argued, 'eat human food': rats, mice, badgers, foxes, as well as birds who stole fish meant for human consumption.[54] In 1566 an Act for the Preservation of Grain was passed that offered rewards, to be paid by churchwardens from funds given by farmers, for the killing of certain 'pests': a dead fox was worth twelve pence; polecats and weasels, one penny; otters and hedgehogs, two pence; three rats, or twelve mice were worth one penny.[55] The larger reward for the fox signifies the larger amount of destruction a fox could cause. Where a mouse might eat grain, a fox could eat chickens and lambs.

It is the activities of the fox as predator that help to give it its reputation as the greatest vermin of all, and this has an impact on the huntsman's attitude towards the animal. The original quarry in the hunt was the deer; however, by the late seventeenth century the number of deer in England was in decline because of the combined forces of poaching and the 'destruction of the forest cover and the deer parks that held the deer'.[56] The huntsmen shifted their focus to the fox, an animal that had previously been hunted on foot. As this process of transition from deer to fox was undertaken, so, Garry Marvin notes, 'those who participated in the event conferred a different status on [the fox] . . . Hunting with hounds was regarded as an essentially noble enterprise; for the quarry to have been a contemptible creature would have been discordant with this image.'[57]

One of the sources of an alternative status for the fox was the beast fable. In texts from the medieval Reynard tales and beyond, the fox was represented as being wily, cunning, and highly intelligent. According to one twelfth-century bestiary, the fox is

> a fraudulent and ingenious animal. When he is hungry and nothing turns up for him to devour, he rolls himself in red mud so that he looks as if he were stained with blood. Then he throws himself on the ground and holds his breath, so that he positively does not breathe. The birds, seeing that he is not breathing, and that he looks as if he were covered with blood with his tongue hanging out, think he is dead and come down to sit on him. Well, thus he grabs them and gobbles them up.

The following line reads, 'The Devil has the nature of the same.'[58] This is clearly not an animal to underestimate. Four hundred years later a similar image of the fox is in place. In Geffrey Whitney's *A Choice of Emblemes* of 1586, for example, one emblem entitled '*Fraus meretur fraudem*' ('fraud merits fraud') represents the wily fox outwitting the king of beasts:

> The Lion old that could not get his prey,
> By swift pursuit, as he had done of late:
> Did feign him sick, and in his den did stay,
> And preyed on those that came to see his state:
> At length, the fox his duty to declare,
> Came to the door, to know how he did fare.
>
> Who answered, 'sick, my old beloved friend;
> Come in and see, and feel my pulses beat.'
> To whom, quoth he, 'I dare not now intend
> Because these steps some secret mischief threat:
> For all I see have gone into thy den,
> But none I find that have returned again.'[59]

The deductive logic exercised by the fox saves it from the lion's jaws. Other animals, it would appear, are not so clever. It is from these different fabled representations of the fox that the alternative image of the animal emerges, and, by the end of the seventeenth century, as the stocks of deer are in decline, the new quarry is presented as simultaneously, and paradoxically, verminous and a worthy opponent.

Marvin notes that in contemporary Britain there are 'some 200 registered fox-hunts . . . each with its defined area, and approximately 250,000 people regularly participate, either on foot or on horseback in the event.' The hunting season runs from early autumn to early spring, and hunts go out during this time at least twice a week. More than one fox can be killed during a day's hunting.[60] The reasons for the continuation of hunting – now more than ever under threat as it is – are particularly important for the maintenance of the sport, and the ambivalent meaning of the fox that emerged in the early modern period plays its part. Contemporary hunts-men and women are involved, so they argue, in a form of 'pest control', and they will cite farmer's stories of lost lambs as evidence to support the continued need to keep the fox population under control. But the concept of foxes as vermin is problematic in two ways. Firstly, a survey carried out in 1993 by the field sports journal *The Field* (a defender of fox hunting) showed that 'sheep farmers felt they lost, on average, only 1 per cent of lambs to foxes'. Another survey, from 1997 proposed that 'between 0.5 per cent and 3 per cent of otherwise viable lambs may be taken by foxes, but that the economic losses as a result of this level of predation are low compared with other causes of mortality'. As the survey team at Bristol University suggests, 'foxes do not warrant their reputation as major pests of agriculture'.[61]

The second problem with the 'vermin defence' is that it goes against the 'nobility' of the 'sport' itself. If hunting is merely pest control, why all the ritual? Something else must be going on, and we can look at Donna Haraway's answer to the question 'What qualities did it take to make an animal "game"?' to begin to see both an ambivalence in the relationship with the fox, and some clear connections, paradoxical as it might seem, between the guided person's relation to their guide dog, and the hunter's relation to their quarry. Haraway argues that 'One answer [to the question] is similarity to man, the ultimate quarry, a worthy opponent. The ideal quarry is the "other," the natural self.'[62] Likewise, Marvin writes that the huntsman, once a scent is lost, 'should use all his years of experience to think like a fox'.[63] The difference between human and animal – huntsman and quarry – is dismissed as the huntsman attempts to comprehend what the fox is thinking; how this other being might be dealing with the situation. Intelligent disobedience might not be an inappropriate term to use for the fox's actions in escaping from the pack of hounds.

It is a necessary part of hunting that the object of the hunt – the fox – has a status that is equal to the nature of the hunt itself. And so the fox has two beings: it is vermin (other) and it is worthy opponent (self). Hunting must maintain both of these narratives simultaneously. There must be a reason for encouraging a pack of hounds to tear a living creature to death, and there must be a grandeur in the ritual. If the reason for hunting is lost – and in the current climate the loss of 'reason' becomes more and more significant – then the hunting itself might be lost. But if the reason really is vermin control, there would appear to be no more nobility in fox hunting than in rat catching. Hunters, it seems, need it both ways.

But the true paradox here lies, perhaps, in the huntsman's relation to the fox. This animal is objectified as vermin and simultaneously given intelligence; it is both a thing and a thinking being. And these oppositions do not cancel each other out. Rather than collapsing the boundaries between hunter and hunted, cleverness – the fox's capacity to evade the pack – makes the fox 'fair game'. The fox is hunted because it can escape the hunt.

In this sense, the ethical claims for proof of animal intelligence may not be so powerful after all. The huntsman requires intelligence in the animal he will destroy, that is the point of the destruction. So naturalized is our belief in animals' inferiority that overturning it will take more than the correction of factual inaccuracy; more than a recognition that there exists in animals a form of intelligence not unlike our own. An animal, it seems, could be a genius, but it would still be an animal. Any claims that humans are the only intelligent beings, and that intelligence is a way of judging whether animals are to be included or excluded from our human community are false. The judgments, it would seem, have already been made. An animal is an animal is an animal, whatever its mental capacity, and the human is always the only thinking animal. An irony, if ever there was one.

The paradoxical (and, of course, cruel) relationship with the fox that can be traced in hunting lays bare, I think, many of the other confusions that persist in our relationships with animals. They are pets and consumer goods; desired objects and dissected subjects; instinctual machines and cultured beings. So, it might seem that an attempt to live in a benign relationship with animals is an impossible one. If we can only see through our own eyes; if we are always-already going to regard animals as other than us – on the basis of their lack of language, of (human) intellect, and so on – and if there is a possibility that, even while claiming intelligence we can continue to use them as objects, then it would seem that the kind of ambivalences outlined in this book are just the way things are, and the way they will always be. We can attempt to make improvements in our treatment of animals, but the underlying principle of the relationship remains one of dominion: the use of anaesthetics during experiments clearly allows for the animal's experience of the experiment to be lessened, but, of course, the experiments go on. There might, however, be an alternative. We can turn to the world of visual art, and find not only a history that appears to mirror the wider cultural attitudes that have been traced in this book, but also something like an alternative way of living with animals.

Painting Another Picture

The objectification of the animal in art can be traced in a number of ways and across a wide historical span. In medieval and Renaissance art, for example, animals were often emblematic; that is, they represented something other than themselves, something human. As Paul Hardwick has noted of the 'Monkeys' Funeral' in the early fourteenth-century Pilgrimage Window of York Minster, this window offers an image of the Assumption, rather than an image of monkeys as such. However, the use of monkeys might seem to be a dangerous, not to say blasphemous, depiction of the Virgin, but Hardwick argues that the image presents the importance of aspiration: 'as the ape, lacking human nature, still mimics humans, so must man, although lacking divinity, mimic the divine'.[64] We humans are taught to yearn for godliness by portraying fictional animals longing for human-ness. Their inferiority is a crucial element of our sense of our own superiority, and as such the stained glass window does not really represent animals at all. Similarly, in the Renaissance visual representations of animals, while attempting something closer to verisimilitude, were also exhibiting something perceived to be more important than the animals themselves. As Claudia Lazzaro argues, 'the representations of animals . . . domesticate the force of nature'.[65] Humans represent animals only in order to represent human power over animals. A visual representation (whether a painting, stained glass window or sculpture) of a wild animal is an image of a wild animal under human control. Framing, in this sense, equates to caging.

This was not the only mode of representation, however. Rather than only using animals to speak of something other than animals, artists also used representations to think about the animals themselves. Perhaps the most famous intervention in this aspect of visual art is William Hogarth's *The Four Stages of Cruelty* (1751). This series of four prints traces the moral decline of the anti-hero Tom Nero, and in *The Second Stage of Cruelty* Nero is represented, in Diana Donald's words, 'aim[ing] violent blows with his thick whip handle at the head of his horse, which has fallen and broken its leg; its staring ribs, the great sore on its chest rubbed by the harness, its distended tongue, tell their own story of dreadful ill treatment, and its tears testify to a sensibility greater than that of its human tormentor'. In his 'autobiographical notes', Hogarth explains that 'the prints were engraved with the hope of, in some degree, correcting that barbarous treatment of animals, the very sight of which renders the streets of our metropolis so distressing to every feeling mind'.[66] Donald reads Hogarth's print as having an important influence on nineteenth-century representations of cruelty to animals. As she shows, in the fight for improved animal welfare in London campaigners found their clearest – and most arresting – representations in the medium of the visual arts: Lewis Gompertz, Secretary of the Society for the Prevention of Cruelty to Animals (later RSPCA) wrote in 1852 that in images 'cruelty is picturesquely brought home to our own doors and hearts'.[67] Paradoxically, you might think, it seemed easier to turn away from the real cruelty in the streets than the representation of cruelty in popular magazines.

This ethical inflection in representations of animals has continued into contemporary culture. In his book *The Postmodern Animal* Steve Baker examines the ways in which contemporary art uses and thinks about animals. Looking at the work of the collaborative artists Olly and Suzi, Baker argues that they 'have sought to make pieces which reflect their immediate encounters and interactions with animals in the wild'. Rather than merely representing animals, their images include the animal's own interventions. These interventions include a shark biting off the corner of the artists' image of a shark that has been thrown into the water, and bears and elephants leaving prints on the artists' work. Baker notes also the 'exceptional cases, where the "artistic interaction" did not go entirely to plan'. These, he writes, 'include a leopard dragging a painting away and destroying it, and a rhinoceros eating a whole piece'. For these two artists, Baker writes, 'the animal is a reminder of the limits of human understanding and influence, but also of the value of working at those limits. The very existence of dangerous wild animals "keeps us in check", they state, and serves to warn that humans (including artists) are "not the boss of everything".'[68] This is work that is attempting to represent animals in a very different way. Animals do not symbolize something else, something human; nor are they domesticated in representation, rather animals emerge as animals. In Olly and Suzi's work we have, perhaps, an attempt to represent the impossibility of the human gaze 'capturing' animals, and we see animals escaping from the conventions of art, even destroying those conventions. Olly and Suzi's animals create 'art' by destroying human representations: it is the interaction, captured in Greg Williams' photographs, that records the animals' artistic power. But Olly and Suzi's images offer only one version of how an animal might be present in visual art. Another way of thinking about this issue is to turn to attempts to analyse artistic creation by animals themselves.

In 1956 Desmond Morris was appointed director of the film unit of London Zoo. As part of his remit Morris produced *Zootime*, a weekly television programme that had as its 'mascot' Congo, a one-year-old wild-born chimpanzee. Each week Congo's 'latest exploits' were broadcast to the nation. Morris had read of experimental work discussing painting by chimpanzees, and he decided to see how Congo would take to drawing. His experiments met with great popular acclaim, and film of the chimp drawing created further interest in the art world. In September 1957 24 of Congo's paintings were shown at the Institute of Contemporary Art in London in an exhibition entitled 'Primitivism'.[69] In 1962 Morris's book, *The Biology of Art* appeared, in which he presented 'a scientific investigation of the origins of aesthetics'. Morris records three different reactions to the seriousness with which he dealt with ape art: 'some were angry, some amused and some intrigued'. In response to the anger of some critics, writing almost 40 years later, Morris said of his 'ape painter', 'he is not a joke, he is not a great artist . . . he is just at the threshold of art, struggling to pass over into that fascinating world of visual exploration that fills our human art galleries and the walls of our houses with such exciting images'.[70] At the threshold of art: this creature can tell us about the origins of art, about artistic production that, in Thierry Lenain's words, 'became more complex only with the advent of the human species'.[71] Just as Robert Yerkes looked to primates to understand the human without culture, so Morris looked to the chimpanzee to find the origins of art.

In his more recent study of monkey painting, Lenain, rather than regarding the primate work as a possible origin, notes some key differences between human and non-human artistic creation. If a human work of art 'is a thing created by a process whose aim is to confer on it a special aesthetic presence', then monkey painting is somewhat different. Lenain writes, 'it is not aimed at creating a tangible object that will have a continuing visible presence after the act of producing is over. Monkeys are totally indifferent to their paintings the moment they are finished.' Later in his study Lenain argues that 'monkey art is primarily an aspect of play. It provides a classic example of those activities termed by Desmond Morris as "self-gratifying", and characterized by being triggered without any very definite stimulus and ceasing without the achievement of any particular goal (beyond the play activity itself).'[72] In this sense, it would seem that, while Jane Goodall and her colleagues are finding regional variation in ape culture, that culture does not include art as we understand that term. The aesthetic object that communicates some kind of meaning is not something that is produced by primates.

Does this then reveal apes as failed humans? Lenain writes that 'The natural reaction of a spectator when faced with a monkey painting is to try to understand it through an aesthetic value system contructed from his experience of human art.' Ape art can only be assessed as human art, because we lack other categories, and as such might fail (as some of the critics of Morris's work show). The only alternative category that we might have would be to term these chimpanzee productions 'paintings', a term that does not attempt to invoke the more aesthetic category 'art', and describes rather than evaluates the product. But this, of course, would leave (human) art untouched by animals. Ape art (if such we are to term it) therefore requires a new and different kind of response. We are not assessing the qualities of verisimilitude – ape art is, on the whole, not representational. Nor are we assessing the choice of materials in the same way that we might with a human artist. As Lenain notes, 'ape painting is captive painting', the ape does not choose its own materials as a human artist would; it is given to them by a human.[73] This would seem to close-off monkey painting as a possible place to find a new, more positive relation with animals. If sign language experiments force the apes into the position of failed humans, and if experiments on animal intelligence often look for what is not there in order not to find it, and so leave humanity comfortable in its position of superiority, monkey painting experiments do not seem to offer anything new. But this might be because we are looking at them wrongly. What if we were to position ourselves with the Austrian artist, Arnulf Rainer, and to attempt to learn from animals, rather than to side with Karl Krall in his disciplined attempts to teach his horses? What would happen to monkey painting then? In Arnulf Rainer's experiments with chimpanzees in the late 1970s an alternative relationship with animals emerges, an alternative relationship that reveals a gulf between humans and animals that might itself be a way forward.

For Rainer, the chimpanzee artist has a kind of 'sovereign . . . sense of the unadulterated mark.' In Thierry Lenain's words, 'the monkey is the only producer of pictures who imitates nothing and nobody and recognizes only the unadulterated pleasure of the disruptive mark.' Where a human artist attempts to represent – perhaps abstractly or symbolically – the chimpanzee merely paints. There is no intervention of anything beyond the experience of the painting itself: this is, if you like, art for art's sake at its most extreme. The apparent 'purity' of the animals' art was made clear in the works that emerged from Rainer's experiments (see opposite). He produced fifteen pieces during his work with the chimpanzees: 'each . . . consists of a chimpanzee painting fixed to the sheet on which Rainer painted his imitation'. Where the chimp's paintings were 'straightforward and clear', however, Rainer's imitations were 'fuzzy, tangled webs of lines, completely illegible, almost to the point of hysteria'.[74] What looked like it should be a simple reversal, with the monkey painter imitated by the human-monkey painter, revealed instead the impossibility of painting like a monkey.

But if art is the realm of the human, Rainer's experiment presents two problems. First, a monkey should not be able to produce 'art', and the fact that it does shows how far our categories fail us. Because we are unable to view the monkey's work as anything other than art, we reveal how far our categorization is based upon culture rather than nature. Secondly, because of the animal's so-called simpler mode of being (that is, natural rather than cultural; instinctual rather than rational), the human must surely be able to reproduce its productions. After all, we are superior. Rainer's failed attempts at imitation again show this idea to be problematic.

What Rainer's work shows, then, is that when we turn to look another way, when we reverse the normal order that sees us attempting to assess the animal's capacity to be like us, and ask to learn from animals, we find something very different. We find, in fact, a limitation to our own sense of power and dominion. Despite being a figure of imitation from classical times,[75] the ape, we realize, does not in fact ape us, it is itself. This is something different, of course, but also, distant, unobtainable.

This is the lesson, I think, that emerges from the place of animals in art. Moving from the emblematic to the more realist depiction, animals were domesticated in visual representation. An attempt was then made to turn this medium against itself, to use it to speak of the objectification of animals. In more recent work it is when art recognizes its own limitations in the way it represents animals that something other emerges: a destruction of the valued human objects, and a destruction of human power. Where Karl Krall taught his horses to be human-like and thought he had achieved his aim only to find his work disproved, Arnulf Rainer attempted to learn from the chimpanzee and found his imitations failed to imitate truly. The moral of this story, surely, is that animals are different from humans. This seems to be an incredibly simple conclusion, but actually, I hope it represents a development. Much of our time is spent thinking about animals as failed or nearly-humans: can they use sign language? are they intelligent? can they make judgments? It would seem logical, perhaps, to begin to try and think about them as animals.

Conclusion

We should think about animals as animals . . .

Throughout this book I have been looking in part at many of the difficulties that we, humans, face when attempting to represent and describe animals. Our language creates and gives meaning to our world, and animals become subsumed into that world because we lack another language with which to represent them. The choice, as I see it, is a simple one: we acknowledge the limitations of our own perspective, but simultaneously accept that what we can achieve with those limitations is important and worthwhile, even if it is only the best that we can do. Or we acknowledge the limitations and from that perspective give up the attempt to discuss animals, and thus exclude from our world those beings that, in great part, have always been used to imagine what it is that we humans are. We would, by our refusal, undercut our own sense of our difference from the other beings in the world, something that has always lain at the heart of our self-perception. My decision has been to go for the former option.

But the logic of both of the possibilities is one that we need to remain aware of. We are simultaneously tied-to and separated from animals. There are a couple of ways of using this conception of our relationship with animals. In the first we must constantly be aware of this paradox as we think about, and represent animals to ourselves and others. We must have in our minds the fact that our perception is based upon our limitations, and the fact that their lives exceed our abilities to think about them. The second way of using this awareness of our simultaneous links to and separations from animals is to apply it to the ways in which we live with them. From this perspective eating meat, consuming the flesh of animals, enacts our separation from animals, but at the same time commemorates our close connection with them in the fact that animal flesh can be taken into human flesh. To have both of these possibilities in place concurrently is logically flawed, in that what is for consumption is an object, not another subject (cannibalism – eating a fellow subject – is a crime, we should remember), but what can become part of us can be converted into us in some fundamental way. If the logic is flawed – and the role of cannibalism as both reason for eating animals, and reason for not eating animals might hint towards illogicality – that has wider ramifications, as logic, this exercise of our reason, is, of course, what is often used to separate us from animals in the first place. The contradictions in our relationships with animals shift from the lived relation to what might be termed the 'thought relation', and it seems that naming animals as 'animal' simultaneously protects us from the contradictions in our relationships with them, and creates those relationships. These simultaneous possibilities bring with them all kinds of difficulties, most of which we remain blissfully unaware of.

And this leads to perhaps the most obvious issue of all, one which I have not mentioned so far in this book: the word 'animal' itself. I have used it throughout to refer to creatures that are not human. Other writers have used other words: 'beast' is sometimes used as an always already moralizing representation. More descriptive (as opposed to evaluative) is the term the 'human animal', with its other, the 'nonhuman animal'. What does this shift in terminology represent? Is it just post-Darwinian political correctness that sees humans signalled as animals? Does the 'nonhuman' aspect of this new nomenclature enhance the status of animals, or merely reinforce the sense that the primary creature of research is always the human, with the animal distinguished from this originary term with a designation of 'non', not being?

This might seem like a discussion that is heading off into the hinterland of philology, but it carries with it some issues that are central to any way of living with and thinking about animals. In an essay on being human, 'The Animal That Therefore I Am (More to Follow)', Jacques Derrida writes:

> Whenever 'one' says, 'The Animal,' each time a philosopher, or anyone else says, 'The Animal' in the singular and without further ado, claiming thus to designate every living thing that is held not to be man . . . each time the subject of that statement, this 'one,' this 'I' does that he utters an *asinanity* [*bêtise*]. He avows without avowing it, he declares, just as a disease is declared by means of a symptom, he offers up for diagnosis that statement, 'I am uttering an *asinanity*.' And this 'I am uttering an *asinanity*' should confirm not only the animality that he is disavowing but his complicit, continued and organized involvement in a veritable war of the species.[1]

Where, in Genesis, Adam named the animals and thus subjected them to his dominion, so, it would seem, we continue something similar every time we name the multiplicity of nonhumans with whom we share our world under the singular term 'the animal'. As well as this, the term produces a relation as much as it signifies one: it is constitutive of two things: the distinction of human from animal, and the animality – *bêtise* – of humans. Again, a logical nightmare.

Derrida highlights the danger of over-generalizing with the singular, 'the Animal', and goes on, adding emotive weight to his statement:

> Confined within this catch-all concept, within this vast encamp-ment of the animal, in this general singular, within the strict enclosure of this definite article ('the Animal' and not 'animals'), as in a virgin forest, a zoo, a hunting or fishing ground, a paddock or an abattoir, a space of domestication, are *all the living things* that man does not recognize as his fellows, his neighbors, or his brothers. And that is so in spite of the infinite space that separates the lizard from the dog, the protozoon from the dolphin, the shark from the lamb, the parrot from the chimpanzee, the camel from the eagle, the squirrel from the tiger or the elephant from the cat, the ant from the silkworm or the hedgehog from the echidna. I interrupt my nomenclature and call Noah to help insure that no one gets left on the ark.[2]

This is an extraordinarily powerful argument. It is hard to deny that 'the animal', the general singular with its definite article, wipes out all difference apart from the difference of the named from the namers. 'The animal' becomes, I think, a ghostly presence, a phantom, not a real animal at all; in fact, animals as such might disappear behind this smoke-screen. I am reminded of an argument from a very different context.

In his work on ethnic identities Stuart Hall has argued that the phrase 'the black experience', used to signify the experience of all non-white people, has become hegemonic; that is, it has come to represent as natural what is, in fact, ideological. The ideological work of the phrase is in its representation as the same, as stereotypical, what is in reality varied, distinct. Hall argues that the phrase merely repeats what is central to racist pronouncements: as he says, 'after all, it is one of the predicates of racism that "you can't tell the difference because they all look the same"'. Hall's work addresses what he terms 'the extraordinary diversity of subjective positions, social experiences and cultural identities which compose the category "black"'. If we do not recognize this, he argues, we will also fail to recognize that '"black" is essentially a politically and culturally *constructed* category which cannot be grounded in a set of fixed trans-cultural or tran-scendent racial categories and which therefore has no guarantees in nature'.[3]

The link between abuses of people from ethnic minorities and animals is an uncomfortable one, and is one that has been used to devalue the lives of both, as Marjorie Spiegel has shown her aptly titled book, *The Dreaded Comparison*.[4] But we can also find a more positive way of recognizing the links between the ways in which these two groups have been and are repre-sented. Hall's assertion of the constructedness of the category 'the black experience' can be translated to the concept 'the animal'. Rather than regarding animals as naturally other we can come to understand that they are always *constructed* as other, but that those constructions come to seem natural, true. When we define the human, as we so often do, it is to animals that we constantly turn. What qualities, we ask, do we have that animals lack? We search, and we find those qualities, but in that searching, as Nietzsche noted, we are also *making* the things we want to find; we are putting them there in the first place. 'Look,' we say, 'they cannot speak,' ignoring the fact that animals manage to communicate within their own species perfectly well, and also ignoring the fact that we cannot communi-cate with them as much as they cannot communicate with us. The generalization allows for a blanket assumption to arise that blocks out not only difference but also the constitution of that difference.

But, of course, I need to defend my use of the singular, 'animal' – it is the title of the book after all, and deliberately so. I have constructed all nonhuman life as the same. I have dismissed, through bringing into the same discussion all sorts of different animals, the uniqueness of all except the human. How, with the power of the arguments of Derrida and Hall in front of me, can I defend this?

I do not dispute that Derrida and Hall are right; I agree that the singular – 'the animal' - can have the effect of deadening differences. But, actually, that has been a part of my project here. I want to make the word 'animal' in all of its singularity an uncomfortable one. I want to argue that the abstract term is exactly what is both necessary, and deeply problematic in a culture where meat eating, pet ownership, animal experimentation and anthropomorphic children's books all sit comfortably together. These very different spheres simultaneously seem to refuse the abstract notion of 'the animal', by having within them such very different relations with those nonhumans. But at the same time as specific lived relations seem to dismiss the possibility of thinking about animals in general, our relationship with these contradictions often also works on the basis of that very singular. That is, we live in a world in which animals have many functions: as individualized pets, as cellophane wrapped meat, as figures of desire and fantasy, as tools of research, as sharers of our capacities, as completers of 'incomplete' humans. But, even with these multiple roles, we cling onto a singular, we work with it, we speak it, we think with it: in all of these ways, as Walter Benjamin proposed, we consume it. But what if we were to take seriously questions like: is the pet an animal? Does animal experimentation invoke the same kinds of anthropomorphism as children's literature? Can the learning processes of a dog, a chimpanzee and a pigeon be used to highlight links between those animals, and between those animals and humans that might not otherwise be perceived? What if we attempted to address those questions, and so many others? One result might be, I hope, that the diversity of not only animals, but of our relationships with them, would be brought to the fore. If this was the case, the singular – 'animal' – might cease to have meaning, and our use of it would become more and more difficult to sustain. On that basis, we would have really thought about how it is that we live with animals, and would have had to name those ways. We would emerge as owners, eaters, wearers, vivisectors, trainers, users, hunters. But we would also emerge as lovers, protectors, communicators, observers, pupils. The question as to whether we could continue to have the subjects of both of these lists framed (caged?) under one term might then emerge as a pressing one. By simultaneously using and laying bare the concept 'animal' as a cover-all for a disconcertingly wide range of relations, I hope to have underlined the discomfort, the variety and the limitations of those relations. And from this, perhaps, it is not only the concept, but the lived relations that might come under scrutiny.

If we are forced to recognize that the dogs we live with, the cows we eat, the chimpanzees we watch on television, the mice we attempt to eradicate, the lions we cage, the mink we wear and the rats we experiment upon are all linked under the term 'animal' might that not make what we section off in our worlds impossible to separate? How can we continue to treat so variously cruelly and kindly what we conceptualize as the same? Doesn't the impossibility of thinking in terms of 'the animal' spring from a recognition of the impossibility of living with them as we do?

References

Introduction

1 Walter Benjamin, 'Gloves', from *One-Way Street* (1925–6), in *One-Way Street and Other Writings*, trans. Edmund Jephcott and Kingsley Shorter (London, 1997), pp. 50–51.

2 See M. B. McMullan, 'The Day the Dogs Died in London', *The London Journal*, XXIII/1 (1998), pp. 32–40.

3 Norman Friedman, *Form and Meaning in Fiction* (Athens, GA, 1975), p. 289.

4 Annabelle Sabloff, *Reordering the Natural World: Humans and Animals in the City* (Toronto, 2001), p. 23 and *passim*.

5 *Ibid.*, pp. 149 and 170.

6 John Moore, *A Mappe of Man's Mortalitie* (London, 1617), p. 9.

7 Lynn White Jr, 'The Historical Roots of our Ecological Crisis', *Science*, CLV/3767 (10 March 1967), pp. 1205 and 1206.

8 F. B. Welbourn, 'Man's Dominion', *Theology*, LXXVIII/665, p. 565.

9 On this issue see Harriet Ritvo, *The Animal Estate: The English and Other Creatures in the Victorian Age* (London, 1990), pp. 205–42.

10 Theologian Andrew Linzey has proposed a way of reading Christian ideas that allows for a more egalitarian relationship with animals. See, for example, his *Animal Gospel: Christian Faith as Though Animals Mattered* (London, 1998).

11 James L. Westcoat Jr, 'The "Right of Thirst" for Animals in Islamic Law:
A Comparative Approach', in Jennifer Wolch and Jody Emel, eds, *Animal Geographies: Place, Politics, and Identity in the Nature–Culture Borderlands* (London, 1998), p. 263.

12 Peter Harvey, *An Introduction to Buddhism: Teachings, History and Practices* (Cambridge, 1990), pp. 202, 197 and 198.

13 Florin Deleanu, 'Buddhist "Ethology" in the Pâli Canon: Between Symbol and Observation', *The Eastern Buddhist*, n.s. XXXII/2 (2000), p. 85.

14 Charles Darwin, *The Origin of Species By Means of Natural Selection*, ed. J. W. Burrow (London, 1968), pp. 459–60.

15 Cited in J. R. Lucas, 'Wilberforce and Huxley: A Legendary Encounter', *The Historical Journal*, XXII/2 (1979), p. 314.

16 Matthew Chapman, 'Sermon Under the Mount', *The Guardian* (4 November 2000), review section, p. 3.

17 See Stephen Jay Gould, 'Genesis vs. Geology', *The Atlantic Monthly*, 250/3 (September 1982), pp. 10–17.

18 Frans de Waal, *The Ape and the Sushi Master: Cultural Reflections by a Primatologist* (London, 2001), p. 116.

19 H. G. Wells, *The Island of Doctor Moreau* (Harmondsworth, 1962), pp. 103 and 104.

20 *Ibid*., pp. 138–9.

One: Visible and Invisible: Questions of Recognition

1 From 'Apollo Expeditions to the Moon', Chapter 2.2, www.hq.nasa.gov/office/pao/History/SP-350/ch-2-2.htm, accessed 22 August 2000.

2 'Animal Astronauts', www.vibrationdata.com/space/Animals, accessed 23 August 2000.

3 Donna Haraway, *Primate Visions: Gender, Race, and Nature in the World of Modern Science* (London, 1992), p. 138.

4 'MR-2: Ham Paves the Way', www.hq.nasa.gov/office/pao/History/SP-

4201/ch10-3.htm, accessed 22 August 2000.

5 In his record of an experiment on pain in an immobilized monkey (discussed in Chapter Two) Richard Ryder records 'baring of teeth' as one of the responses of the animals that were subjected to 'intense electric shock through their tails'. Richard Ryder, *Victims of Science: The Use of Animals in Research*, revd edn (London, 1983), p. 65.

6 See Lilliane Bodson, 'Motivation for Pet-Keeping in Ancient Greece and Rome', in Anthony Podberscek, Elizabeth S. Paul and James A. Serpell, eds, *Companion Animals and Us* (Cambridge, 2000), pp. 27–41.

7 Keith Thomas, *Man and the Natural World: Changing Attitudes in England, 1500–1800* (London, 1983), p. 95.

8 See W. G. Hoskins, 'The Rebuilding of Rural England, 1570–1640', *Past and Present*, IV (1956), pp. 44–59.

9 Edward Topsell, *The Historie of Foure-Footed Beastes* (London, 1607), pp. 171–2.

10 William Lambard, *Eirenarcha; or of the Offices of Justices of the Peace in Foure Bookes* (London, 1592), p. 268.

11 Noël Sweeney, *Animals and Cruelty and Law* (Bristol, 1990), p. 25.

12 On the history of deodand legislation, see Erica Fudge, *Perceiving Animals: Humans and Beasts in Early Modern English Culture* (Basingstoke, 2000), pp. 121–5.

13 Peter Hillmore, 'Have We Gone Barking Mad?', *The Observer* (27 August 1995), p. 21.

14 Thomas, *Man and the Natural World*, p. 114.

15 William Shakespeare, *The Two Gentlemen of Verona*, II.iii.5–6, in Stanley Wells and Gary Taylor, eds, *The Complete Works of William Shakespeare* (Oxford, 1988).

16 Thomas, *Man and the Natural World*, p. 115.

17 Susan Stanton, 'It was a Simple, Low-Key Wedding', www.jacksonville.com/tu-online/stories/100700/nes_4268511.html, accessed 23 November 2000.

18 *Ibid*.

19 Marc Shell, 'The Family Pet', *Representations*, xv (1986), p. 126.

20 Marjorie Garber, *Dog Love* (London, 1997), p. 32.

21 *Ibid.*, p. 17.

22 Shell, 'Family Pet', p. 132: his use of structuralist ideas is most evident when he writes of the 'taboo on bestiality', p. 141.

23 Sigmund Freud, *Jokes and their Relation to the Unconscious* (1905), trans. James Strachey (London, 1960), p. 129.

24 Carol Adams, *The Sexual Politics of Meat: A Feminist-Vegetarian Critical Theory* (Cambridge, 1990), pp. 40 and 93.

25 Robert Malcolmson and Stephanos Mastoris, *The English Pig: A History* (London, 1998).

26 Roger A. Caras, *A Perfect Harmony: The Intertwining Lives of Animals and Humans throughout History* (New York, 1996), p. 185.

27 Steve Connor, 'The Milk of Human Kindness', www.fortunecity.com/ greenfield/ shell/5/trans.htm, accessed 23 November 2000.

28 Ted Benton and Simon Redfearn, 'The Politics of Animal Rights – Where is the Left?', *New Left Review*, 215 (1996), p. 51.

29 Survey results recorded by the Vegetarian Society, www.vegsoc.org/info/ statveg90.html, accessed 11 December 2001.

30 Anita Guerrini, 'A Diet for the Sensitive Soul: Vegetarianism in Eighteenth-century Britain', *Eighteenth-Century Life*, XXIII/2 (1999), p. 36; see also Colin Spencer, *The Heretic's Feast: A History of Vegetarianism* (London, 1994).

31 Bob Roberts and Geoffrey Lakeman, 'Thank God: Joy as Blair saves Phoenix from the Slaughtermen', *The Mirror* (26 April 2001), p. 4.

32 'The Voice of The Mirror', *The Mirror* (26 April 2001), p. 1.

33 Quoted in Roberts and Lakeman, 'Thank God', p. 5.

34 www.anchor.co.nz/content/butter/faq.htm, accessed 12 January 2001.

35 Statistics from the Vegetarian Society.

36 www.microtime.co.uk/animal/features.htm, accessed 12 January 2001.

37 Jeffrey Alan Ford, 'Appreciate Animals to Pieces with a Knife and Fork', www.detnews.com/editpage/9805/02/comment/comment.htm, accessed 12 January 2001.

38 On the emergence of the animal rights movement in Britain see Hilda Kean, *Animal Rights: Political and Social Change in Britain since 1800* (London, 1998).

39 Ford, 'Appreciate Animals to Pieces'.

40 Peter Singer, *Animal Liberation*, 2nd edn (London, 1990), p. viii.

41 Ryder, *Victims of Science*, p. 5.

42 Singer, *Animal Liberation*, pp. 15–16.

43 *Ibid.*, pp. 165–6.

44 Steve Baker, *Picturing the Beast: Animals, Identity and Representation* (Manchester, 1993), p. 195.

45 Keith Tester, *Animals and Society: The Humanity of Animal Rights* (London, 1991), pp. 16 and 44.

46 Ted Benton, *Natural Relations: Ecology, Animal Rights and Social Justice* (London, 1993), pp. 87 and 93.

47 Tester, *Animals and Society*, p. 42.

48 Benton, *Natural Relations*, pp. 65–6.

49 'Naomi Campbell hasn't got the balls to stick by her principles – or has she?', www.gemini.org.uk/passion/april97/naomi.htm. accessed 15 May 2001.

50 Quoted by Mark Tran, 'Animal Rights Group Fires Model Who Wore Fur at Fashion Show', *The Guardian* (12 March 1997), p. 9.

51 See Frances Elizabeth Baldwin, *Sumptuary Legislation and Personal Regulation in England* (Baltimore, 1926).

52 Julia V. Emberley, *Venus and Furs: The Cultural Politics of Fur* (London, 1998), p. 44.

53 www.furs.com/FUR/furage163.html. Accessed 15 May 2001.

54 'Plea to keep fur on its owners', *The Independent* (31 October 1996), p. 3.

55 Susannah Frankel, 'Fur's big comeback snares supermodel', *The Guardian* (8 March 1997), p. 4.

56 Susannah Barron, 'To Die For', *The Guardian* (26 November 1997), G2, p. 14.

57 Animal Emancipation, 'Fur: The Dying Mythology', excerpted on www.allforanimals.com/november, accessed 15 May 2001.

58 Hilary Alexander, 'Naomi: Pride and Prejudice', *The Daily Telegraph* (10 April 1997), p. 15.

59 Barron, 'To Die For', p. 14.

60 *Ibid.*, p. 14.

61 Emberley, *Venus and Furs*, pp. 2 and 3 (Brody quoted on p. 3).

62 Tom Regan, *The Case for Animal Rights* (London, 1984), p. 359.

63 Jean Baudrillard, 'Simulacra and Simulations', in *Selected Writings*, ed. Mark Poster (Cambridge, 1988), pp. 167, 171 and 172.

64 Christopher Norris, *Uncritical Theory: Postmodernism, Intellectuals and the Gulf War* (London, 1992), pp. 11, 15, 16 and 14.

65 Julia Szabo, 'At the Fur Front', *The Guardian* (13 January 1995), G2, p. 6.

66 Quoted in Frankel, 'Fur's big comeback', p. 4.

67 See Laura Levine, 'Men in Women's Clothing: Anti-theatricality and Effeminization from 1579 to 1642', *Criticism*, XXVIII/2 (1986), pp. 121–43.

68 William Prynne, *Histrio-Mastix: The Players Scourge, or Actors Tragedie* (London, 1633), p. 892.

69 Thomas Aquinas, *Summa Theologiae*, trans. R. J. Batten (London, 1975), p. 91.

70 Kate Soper, *Humanism and Anti-Humanism*, cited in Neil Badmington, ed., *Posthumanism* (Basingstoke, 2000), p. 2.

71 Jacques Derrida, 'The Animal That Therefore I Am (More to Follow)', trans. David Wills, *Critical Inquiry* 28 (2002), pp. 373–4.

72 Michael Dalton, *The Countrey Justice* (London, 1618), p. 242.

73 Derrida, 'The Animal That Therefore I Am', p. 409.

Two: Real and Symbolic: Questions of Difference

1 On the rise in popularity of dog breeding and competitions see Harriet Ritvo, *The Animal Estate: The English and Other Creatures in the Victorian Age* (London, 1990), pp. 82–121.

2 C. R. Carpenter, 'Approaches to Studies of the Naturalistic Communicative Behavior in Nonhuman Primates', in Thomas A. Seboek and Alexandra Ramsey, eds, *Approaches to Animal Communication* (The Hague, 1969), p. 55.

3 Sigmund Freud, *Totem and Taboo*, trans. James Strachey (London, 1953), pp. 126–7.

4 Karin Lesnik-Oberstein, 'Children's Literature and the Environment', in Richard Kerridge and Neil Sammells, eds, *Writing the Environment:*

Ecocriticism and Literature (London, 1998), p. 208.

5 Kenneth Grahame, *The Wind in the Willows* (London, 1971).

6 Neil Philip, '"The Wind in the Willows": The Vitality of a Classic', in Gillian Avery and Julia Briggs, eds, *Children and their Books: A Celebration of the Work of Iona and Peter Opie* (Oxford, 1989), p. 299.

7 Chris Baldick, *Concise Dictionary of Literary Terms* (Oxford, 1990), p. 128.

8 Grahame, *The Wind in the Willows*, p. 41.

9 *Ibid.*, p. 123.

10 E. B. White, *Charlotte's Web* (Harmondsworth, 1963), p. 57.

11 Eric Knight, *Lassie Come-Home* (London, 1994), p. 97.

12 *Ibid.*, p. 220.

13 Marjorie Garber, *Dog Love* (London, 1997), p. 59.

14 Knight, *Lassie*, p. 21.

15 Ben Jonson, 'To Penshurst', in *Ben Jonson: The Complete Poems*, ed. George Parfitt (London, 1988), p. 96.

16 Rudd B. Weatherwax and John H. Rothwell, *The Story of Lassie: His Discovery and Training from Puppyhood to Stardom* (London, 1951), pp. 21 and 22.

17 'Rin Tin Tin Films', www.rintintin.org/rin_tin_tin_films, accessed 9 August 2001.

18 Weatherwax and Rothwell, *Story of Lassie*, pp. 23 and 24–5.

19 *Ibid.*, p. 23.

20 *Ibid.*, p. 40.

21 Jonathan Burt, 'The Illumination of the Animal Kingdom: The Role of Light and Electricity in Animal Representation', *Society and Animals*, IX/3 (2001), p. 210.

22 Weatherwax, *Story of Lassie*, p. 29.

23 Ann C. Paietta and Jean L. Kauppila, *Animals on Screen and Radio: An Annotated Bibliography* (London and Metuchen, NJ, 1994), p. 323.

24 Weatherwax, *Story of Lassie*, pp. 71–2.

25 Jerry C. Kutner, 'The Horror of Disney's "Old Yeller"', *Bright Lights Film Journal*, www.brightlightsfilm.com/32/oldyeller1 and 2, accessed 9 August 2001.

26 Dick King-Smith, *The Sheep-Pig* (London, 1999), p. 79.

27 *Ibid.*, p. 115.

28 Estelle Shay, 'From the Mouth of Babe', *Cinefex*, 64 (December 1995), p. 31.

29 Stephen Budianski, *If a Lion Could Talk: Animal Intelligence and the Evolution of Consciousness* (New York, 1998), p. xxi.

30 *The Book of Beasts: Being a Translation from a Latin Bestiary of the Twelfth Century*, ed. and trans. T. H. White (Stroud, 1992), pp. 92–3.

31 Francis Bacon, *The Masculine Birth of Time* (1603), in *The Philosophy of Francis Bacon*, ed. Benjamin Farrington (Liverpool, 1964), p. 69.

32 Francis Bacon, *Valerius Terminus or the Interpretation of Nature* (1603) in *The Works of Francis Bacon*, ed. James Spedding, Robert Leslie Ellis and Douglas Denon Heath (Stuttgart, 1963), vol. III, p. 222.

33 *The Diary of Samuel Pepys*, ed. Robert Latham and William Matthews (London, 1971), vol. V, p. 151; vol. VI, pp. 57 and 84.

34 Andreas-Holger Maehle and Ulrich Tröhler, 'Animal Experimentation from Antiquity to the End of the Eighteenth Century: Attitudes and Arguments', in N. A. Rupke, ed., *Vivisection in Historical Perspective* (London, 1990), p. 15.

35 Dix Harwood, *Love for Animals and How it Developed in Great Britain* (New York, 1928), p. 81.

36 René Descartes, *Meditations*, in *The Philosophical Writings of Descartes*, trans. John Cottingham, Robert Stoothoff and Dugald Murdoch (Cambridge, 1984), vol. II, p. 12.

37 René Descartes, *Discourse on Method*, in *Philosophical Writings*, vol. I, pp. 139–40.

38 L. D. Cohen, 'Descartes and Henry More on the Beast-Machine – A Translation of their Correspondence Pertaining to Animal Automatism', *Annals of Science*, I (1936), pp. 50, 51 and 53.

39 Sir Kenelm Digby, *Two Treatises* (London, 1645), p. 379.

40 White, *Book of Beasts*, p. 53.

41 Maehle and Tröhler, 'Animal Experimentation', p. 15.

42 Gabriel Daniel, *A Voyage to the World of Cartesius* (London, 1692), p. 241.

43 Richard Ryder, *Victims of Science: The Use of Animals in Research*, 2nd edn (London, 1983), p. 12.

44 www.thalidomide.ca, accessed 15 August 2001.

45 Ryder, *Victims of Science*, p. 32.

46 *Ibid.*, cited p. 160.

47 *Ibid.*, pp. 65 and 53.

48 John Cottingham, 'A Brute to Brutes? Descartes' Treatment of Animals', *Philosophy*, 53 (1978), p. 558.

49 Ryder, *Victims of Science*, pp. 67 and 68.

50 'Home Office Statistics on Procedures on Living Animals 1999', www.buav.org.uk, accessed 10 August 2001.

51 Department of Health, 'United Kingdom Xenotransplantation Interim Regulatory Authority (ukxira)', www.doh.gov.uk/ukxira, accessed 15 August 2001.

52 White, *Book of Beasts*, p. 28; *The Book of Secrets of Albertus Magnus*, ed. Michael R. Best and Frank H. Brightman (Oxford, 1973), p. 86.

53 Robert Boyle, *The Method Observed in Transfusing the Blood out of one Animal into Another*, in *The Works of the Honourable Robert Boyle in Six Volumes* (London, 1772), vol. III, p. 150.

54 Anita Guerrini, 'The Ethics of Animal Experimentation in Seventeenth-century England', *Journal of the History of Ideas*, 1/3 (1989), pp. 403–4.

55 Alix Fano, Murry J. Cohen, Marjorie Cramer, Ray Greek, Stephen R. Kaufman, 'Of Pigs, Primates, and Plagues: A Layperson's Guide to the Problems with Animal-to-Human Organ Transplants', Medical Research Modernization Committee, www.mrmcmed.org/pigs, accessed 15 August 2001.

56 F.D.A., 'Fact Sheet on Xenotransplantation', www.fda.gov/backgrounders/xeno, accessed 15 August 2001.

57 Fano et al., 'Of Pigs'.

58 British Union for the Abolition of Vivisection, 'Insight into Xenotransplantation', www.buav.org.uk, accessed 10 August 2001.

59 White, *Charlotte's Web*, p. 164.

60 King-Smith, *The Sheep-Pig*, p. 76.

61 Francis Bacon, *Thoughts and Conclusions on the Interpretation of Nature* (1604), in Benjamin Farringdon, ed., *The Philosophy of Francis Bacon*, p. 74.

62 Cited by Annabelle Sabloff, *Reordering the Natural World: Humans and Animals in the City* (Toronto, 2001), p. 104.

1 Gerd H. Hövelmann, 'Animal "language" research: the perpetuation of some old mistakes', *Semiotica*, 73/3–4 (1989), p. 203.

2 Jan Bondeson, *The Feejee Mermaid and Other Essays in Natural and Unnatural History* (New York, 1999), p. 15.

3 Hövelmann, 'Animal "language" research', p. 210.

4 Nashe quoted in J. O. Halliwell-Phillips, *Memoranda on Love's Labour's Lost, King John, Othello, and on Romeo and Juliet* (London, 1879), p. 52; Richard Brathwaite, *A Strappado for the Divell* (London, 1615), p. 159; Joseph Hall, *Virgidemarum* (London, 1597), p. 62.

5 Gervase Markham, *Cavelarice, Or The English Horseman* (London, 1607), book 8, p. 30.

6 Samuel Rid, *The Art of Jugling or Legerdemaine* (London, 1614), sigs F4v–G1r.

7 Stephen Budiansky, *If a Lion Could Talk: Animal Intelligence and the Evolution of Consciousness* (New York, 1998), pp. xxx and xxxi.

8 Clifford Wilson, 'Smart Animals and Talking Monkeys', *Creation Ex Nihilo*, v/2, (1982), p. 6, reprinted on www.answersingenesis.org/docs/3518.asp?vPrint=1, accessed 24 August 2001.

9 Richard Sorabji, *Animal Minds and Human Morals: The Origin of the Western Debate* (London, 1993), p. 80.

10 Irven M. Resnick and Kenneth F. Kitchell, Jr, 'Albert the Great on the "Language" of Animals', *American Catholic Philosophical Quarterly*, LXX/1 (1996), p. 42.

11 René Descartes, *Discourse on Method* (1637), in *The Philosophical Writings of Descartes*, trans. John Cottingham, Robert Stoothoff and Dugald Murdoch (Cambridge, 1985), vol. I, p. 140.

12 R. Allen Gardner and Beatrice T. Gardner, 'Teaching Sign Language to a Chimpanzee', *Science*, 165 (15 August 1969), pp. 664–72.

13 Jerry H. Gill, *If a Chimpanzee Could Talk and Other Reflections on Language Acquisition* (Tucson, AZ, 1997), pp. 15–16.

14 David Premack, 'Language in Chimpanzee?', *Science*, 172 (21 May 1971), pp. 808–22.

15 E. S. Savage-Rumbaugh, 'Language Acquisition in a Nonhuman Species: Implications for the Debate', *Developmental Psychobiology*, XXIII/7 (1990), pp. 605 and 608–9.

16 H. S. Terrace, L. A. Petitto, R. J. Sanders and T. G. Beaver, 'Can an Ape Create a Sentence?', *Science*, 206 (21 November 1979), pp. 896 and 899.

17 Savage-Rumbaugh, 'Language Acquisition', p. 603.

18 Budiansky, *If a Lion Could Talk*, p. 152.

19 Hövelmann, 'Animal "language" research', pp. 206 and 211.

20 The Gorilla Foundation, 'Mission Statement', www.koko.org, accessed 10 March 2001.

21 The interviews are: www.geocities/Vines/4451/KokoLiveChat.html (Interview on 27 April 1998), and www.freecitymedia.com/KokoText.html (summer 2001), both accessed 22 August 2001.

22 Geocities interview.

23 FreeCityMedia interview.

24 Donna Haraway, *Primate Visions: Gender, Race, and Nature in the World of Modern Science* (London, 1992), pp. 9, 24, 62 and 11.

25 Friedrich Nietzsche, 'On Truth and Lies in a Nonmoral Sense', in Daniel Breazeale, trans. and ed., *Philosophy and Truth: Selections from Nietzsche's Notebooks of the Early 1870s* (Sussex, 1979), pp. 79 and 85–6.

26 Haraway, *Primate Visions*, p. 24.

27 Will Self, *Great Apes* (London, 1997), pp. 245, 385 and 396–7.

28 Frans de Waal, *The Ape and the Sushi Master: Cultural Reflections by a Primatologist* (London, 2001), p. 52.

29 Jane Goodall cited in Jeffrey Masson and Susan McCarthy, *When Elephants Weep: The Emotional Lives of Animals* (London, 1994), p. 12.

30 Robert Hinde, *Ethology*, cited in de Waal, *Ape and the Sushi Master*, p. 37.

31 Matthew Arnold, *Culture and Anarchy* (1869), cited in Francis Mulhern, *Culture/Metaculture* (London, 2000), p. xvi.

32 Edward Tylor, *Primitive Culture*, cited in de Waal, *Ape and the Sushi Master*, p. 215.

33 Raymond Williams, 'Culture is Ordinary', in Ann Gray and Jim McGuigan, eds, *Studying Culture: An Introductory Reader* (London, 1993), p. 6.

34 See David Williams, 'The Right Horse, The Animal Eye – Bartabas and

Théâtre Zingaro', *Performance Research*, V/2 (2000), pp. 29–40.

35 De Waal, *Ape and the Sushi Master*, p. 214.

36 G.W.F. Hegel, *The Philosophy of History*, cited in Henk Wesseling, 'Overseas History', in Peter Burke, ed., *New Perspectives on Historical Writing* (Cambridge, 1992), p. 75.

37 De Waal, *Ape and the Sushi Master*, pp. 200–204.

38 A. Whiten, J. Goodall, W. C. McGrew, T. Nishida, V. Reynolds, Y. Sugiyama, C.E.G. Tutin, R. W. Wrangham and C. Boesch, 'Culture in Chimpanzees', *Science*, 399 (17 June 1999), p. 682.

39 Marian Stamp Dawkins, *Through Our Eyes Only? The Search for Animal Consciousness* (Oxford, 1998), pp. 119 and 120.

40 Lesley J. Rogers, *Minds of Their Own: Thinking and Awareness in Animals* (St Leonards, NSW, 1997), pp. 66–8.

41 Quoted in Budiansky, *If a Lion Could Talk*, p. 104.

42 Noam Chomsky, quoted in George Johnson, 'Chimp Talk Debate: Is It Really Language?' *New York Times* (6 June 1995), Section C, p. 1.

43 Budiansky, *If a Lion Could Talk*, p. 122.

44 Michel Foucault, *The Order of Things* (London, 1989), p. xv.

45 From Guide Dogs for the Blind, 'History', www.gdba.org.uk/aboutus/history.html, accessed 6 November 2001.

46 Guide Dogs for the Blind, Inc., 'Current Program Statistics', and 'An Overview of Guide Dogs for the Blind', www.guidedogs.com/NOPICS/about-stats.htm, and about-overview.htm, accessed 6 November 2001.

47 *Ibid*.

48 Guide Dogs for the Blind, Inc., 'Guide Dog Training: The Phases of Guidework Training', www.guidedogs.com/NOPICS/train-phases.htm, accessed 6 November 2001.

49 Guide Dog Foundation for the Blind Inc., 'Stories of Second Sight', www.guidedog.org/ Pubs/pubs.htm, accessed 6 November 2001.

50 Clinton R. Sanders, 'The Impact of Guide Dogs on the Identity of People with Visual Impairments', *Anthrozoös*, XIII/3 (2000), pp. 134, 137 and 136.

51 Annabelle Sabloff, *Reordering the Natural World: Humans and Animals in the*

City (Toronto, 2001), p. 77.

52 Roger Scruton, *On Hunting* (London, 1998), pp. 73–4.

53 Tom Regan, *The Case for Animal Rights* (London, 1984), p. 354.

54 Mary Fissell, 'Imagining Vermin in Early Modern England', *History Workshop Journal*, 47 (1999), p. 4.

55 8 Eliz.*c*.15 (1566), in *Statutes of the Realm* (London, 1963), vol. IV, pt.1, p. 498.

56 Raymond Carr, *English Fox Hunting: A History* (London, 1976), pp. 22–3.

57 Garry Marvin, 'The Problem with Foxes: Legitimate and Illegitimate killing in the English Countryside', in John Knight, ed., *Natural Enemies: People–Wildlife Conflicts in Anthropological Perspective* (London and New York, 2000), pp. 190 and 192.

58 *The Book of Beasts: Being a Translation from a Latin Bestiary of the Twelfth Century*, ed. and trans. T. H. White (Stroud, 1984), pp. 53–4.

59 Geffrey Whitney, *A Choice of Emblemes, and Other Devices* (London, 1586), p. 210.

60 Marvin, 'The Problem with Foxes', pp. 192–3.

61 *Ibid.*, p. 201.

62 Haraway, *Primate Visions*, p. 31.

63 Marvin, 'The Problem with Foxes', p. 198.

64 Paul Hardwick, 'The Monkeys' Funeral in the Pilgrimage Window, York Minster', *Art History*, XXIII/2 (2000), p. 297.

65 Claudia Lazzaro, 'Animals as Cultural Signs: A Medici Menagerie in the Grotto at Castello', in Claire Farago, ed., *Reframing the Renaissance: Visual Culture in Europe and Latin America, 1450–1650* (New Haven, CT, 1995), p. 203.

66 Diana Donald, '"Beastly Sights": The Treatment of Animals as a Moral Theme in Representations of London, *c*. 1820–1850', *Art History*, XXII/4 (1999), p. 525; *Anecdotes of William Hogarth, Written by Himself*, cited on p. 526.

67 Lewis Gompertz, *Fragments in Defence of Animals* (1852), cited in Donald, 'Beastly Sights', p. 523.

68 Steve Baker, *The Postmodern Animal* (London, 2000), pp. 11, 12 and 16. The image of the shark is on the cover of Baker's book.

69 Thierry Lenain, *Monkey Painting* (London, 1997), pp. 76–93.

70 Desmond Morris, 'Introduction' to Lenain, *Monkey Painting*, p. 7.

71 Lenain, *Monkey Painting*, p. 21.

72 *Ibid.*, pp. 114 and 136.
73 *Ibid.*, pp. 178 and 162.
74 *Ibid.*, pp. 179–80.
75 The classic study of this is H. W. Janson, *Apes and Ape Lore in the Middle Ages and the Renaissance* (London, 1952).

Conclusion

1 Jacques Derrida, 'The Animal That Therefore I Am (More to Follow)', trans. David Wills, *Critical Inquiry* 28 (2002), pp. 399–400.
2 *Ibid.*, p. 402.
3 Stuart Hall, 'New Ethnicities', in *Stuart Hall: Critical Dialogues in Cultural Studies*, ed. David Morley and Kuan-Hsing Chen (London, 1996), pp. 441, 444 and 443.
4 Marjorie Spiegel, *The Dreaded Comparison: Human and Animal Slavery* (London, 1988).

Acknowledgements

I have been given great support throughout the writing of this book by numerous friends and colleagues. My sister Tessa and friend Jonathan Burt both read the whole manuscript and offered invaluable comments and suggestions. They pointed out moments lacking in clarity, and moments replete with stupidity, for which I am grateful. Sections of the book were read by Steve Baker and Garry Marvin. I am extremely indebted to them for their time, ideas, and kindness. References and thoughts were also offered by many friends and colleagues, and I would like to thank in particular my fellow members of the Animal Studies Group, Steve Baker, Jonathan Burt, Diana Donald, Garry Marvin, Robert McKay, Clare Palmer and Chris Wilbert. I am indeed fortunate to have them around. Mary Campbell first told me about Koko, James Knowles shared his knowledge of Inigo Jones, Thierry Lenain was helpful in tracing an illustration, and Rachel Malik, Francis Mulhern, Lawrence Normand and Joanne Winning, my colleagues at Middlesex University, listened with patience and ideas throughout. As well as these people I have been given great help by Rachel Morgan in the Tottenham Campus Library at Middlesex University, and Bobbie Mitchell in the BBC Picture Library. Thanks to them. It goes without saying, of course, that any mistakes in this book are mine.

List of Illustrations